CAMBRIDGE LIBRARY COLLECTION

Books of enduring scholarly value

Cambridge

The city of Cambridge received its royal charter in 1201, having already been home to Britons, Romans and Anglo-Saxons for many centuries. Cambridge University was founded soon afterwards and celebrated its octocentenary in 2009. This series explores the history and influence of Cambridge as a centre of science, learning, and discovery, its contributions to national and global politics and culture, and its inevitable controversies and scandals.

Ancient Cambridgeshire

This work, first published in 1853, grew from a paper describing the crossing of two Roman roads at Cambridge, and the small Roman fort at Grantchester. However, other Roman sites were added to the investigation, and the book came to encompass all the Roman and other ancient roads of Cambridgeshire, as well as the locations where Roman coins and other remains had been found. The author, Charles Cardale Babington (1808–95), is best remembered as the pupil and assistant of John Stevens Henslow and as his successor in the chair of botany at Cambridge. However, Babington was also keenly interested in archaeology, and this fascinating work of local history is the first substantial account of Roman Cambridgeshire, describing not only the courses of the various roads but also finds such as the Roman villa at Comberton, the Roman cemetery at Trumpington, and large numbers of individual coins and other artefacts.

Cambridge University Press has long been a pioneer in the reissuing of out-of-print titles from its own backlist, producing digital reprints of books that are still sought after by scholars and students but could not be reprinted economically using traditional technology. The Cambridge Library Collection extends this activity to a wider range of books which are still of importance to researchers and professionals, either for the source material they contain, or as landmarks in the history of their academic discipline.

Drawing from the world-renowned collections in the Cambridge University Library and other partner libraries, and guided by the advice of experts in each subject area, Cambridge University Press is using state-of-the-art scanning machines in its own Printing House to capture the content of each book selected for inclusion. The files are processed to give a consistently clear, crisp image, and the books finished to the high quality standard for which the Press is recognised around the world. The latest print-on-demand technology ensures that the books will remain available indefinitely, and that orders for single or multiple copies can quickly be supplied.

The Cambridge Library Collection brings back to life books of enduring scholarly value (including out-of-copyright works originally issued by other publishers) across a wide range of disciplines in the humanities and social sciences and in science and technology.

Ancient Cambridgeshire

Or, an Attempt to Trace Roman and Other Ancient Roads that Passed through the County of Cambridge

CHARLES CARDALE BABINGTON

CAMBRIDGE
UNIVERSITY PRESS

CAMBRIDGE
UNIVERSITY PRESS

University Printing House, Cambridge, CB2 8BS, United Kingdom

Cambridge University Press is part of the University of Cambridge.

It furthers the University's mission by disseminating knowledge in the pursuit of
education, learning and research at the highest international levels of excellence.

www.cambridge.org
Information on this title: www.cambridge.org/9781108075572

© in this compilation Cambridge University Press 2014

This edition first published 1853
This digitally printed version 2014

ISBN 978-1-108-07557-2 Paperback

Ancient Cambridgeshire:

OR AN ATTEMPT TO TRACE

ROMAN AND OTHER ANCIENT ROADS

THAT PASSED THROUGH

THE COUNTY OF CAMBRIDGE;

WITH A RECORD

OF THE PLACES WHERE ROMAN COINS
AND OTHER REMAINS HAVE BEEN FOUND.

BY

CHARLES CARDALE BABINGTON, M.A., F.R.S.,

OF ST. JOHN'S COLLEGE.

CAMBRIDGE:
DEIGHTON; MACMILLAN AND CO.
J. W. PARKER AND SON, LONDON.
J. H. PARKER, OXFORD.

M.DCCC.LIII.

Printed at the University Press.

PREFACE.

THE following treatise has gradually increased to its present bulk from a very small origin. It was intended to have consisted only of an account of the Roman roads, which crossed each other at Cambridge to the extent of a few miles on each side of that place; and of a description of the small Roman station or fort at Grantchester. In that form the paper was read to the Cambridge Antiquarian Society, and together with a small and imperfect map, would have been immediately issued to the members, had not circumstances occurred which caused delay. It was then determined to describe all the ancient roads that pass through the county of Cambridge, and slightly trace their farther course to their destination. This led to an examination of the authority upon which some of them were supposed to be ancient, and caused an extensive search to be made for records of the discovery of Roman remains within Cambridgeshire. The whole has resulted in the following treatise, in which an attempt is made to trace all the roads in the district that appear to have been used in early times, pointing out their probable origin; to name all the places where Roman antiquities or coins have

been found, with their authorities; and to describe
the ancient ditches, camps, and other earth-works.

The position of Cambridgeshire on the frontiers
of East Anglia and Mercia, and its consequently disturbed state during much of the Saxon period, has
unfortunately caused it to be very deficient in records
of those centuries, during which we might reasonably
have expected to find the ancient roads and sites
mentioned in charters: as an illustration, reference
may be made to the proof that the so-called "*Cnut's
Dyke*" is older than the time of King Cnut, derived
from its mention, under another of its names, in a
charter of a date anterior to his reign.

Very small pretensions are made to originality,
but in all cases the quotations have been taken from
the works themselves; and by far the greater number
of the facts recorded are now brought together for
the first time. Let it not however be supposed that
all those which exist are here collected; for although,
no labour has been spared in looking for them, it is
highly probable that many have escaped notice. What
has been done, will, however, shew that, in this part
of England, there are few parishes in which Roman
coins may not be found, and that in a very considerable
number there are traces of Roman occupancy in the
form of remains of their fictile manufactures.

The plans which accompany this treatise have
been made with care, and are, it is believed, correct.

The modern parts of the plans of the stations at Cambridge and Grantchester are reduced from Baker's large map of Cambridge; the plan of the station at Bury is derived from an eye-sketch and measurement made by pacing the ground; the villa at Comberton was carefully measured and laid down to scale by my friend the Rev. J. J. Smith.

The general outline of the accompanying map, and the positions of modern places in the county, have been derived from Walker's Map of Cambridgeshire. No modern villages are marked upon it that do not tend in some way to point out the position of sites mentioned in the treatise; but all places are inserted, and their names underlined, at or near to which Roman remains or coins have been found. No modern roads are introduced. An attempt has been made to point out by a different mode of drawing the supposed origin, more or less certain antiquity, and the course of the several ancient roads: the expense of colouring being one which it has been thought better to avoid on account of the small amount of funds at the disposal of the Cambridge Antiquarian Society under the auspices of which body this treatise is published. Only such of the watercourses are given as appeared to be necessary for the purpose of shewing the ancient state of the country or the position of places.

British antiquities, such as celts of stone, palstaves, spear-heads and swords of bronze, beads of glass, &c.,

have occurred, spread over the country in such a manner as not to connect themselves with the modern or Roman sites of habitation, and they are rarely noticed in the following pages, the contents of which are intended to refer to the four centuries of the Roman rule in England.

St John's College,
April 20, 1853.

CONTENTS.

viii

ANCIENT CAMBRIDGESHIRE.

It cannot but afford some cause for astonishment that no separate dissertation concerning the ancient state of the county of Cambridge has been published, as it is impossible not to believe that a learned and populous University must have had very many amongst its members desirous of knowing, and at the same time well qualified to ascertain, the extent to which the county was traversed by roads and settled in the Roman and even in British times. Although no separate, or connected, treatise on this interesting subject exists, there are materials from which a considerable amount of information may be obtained.

The persons to whom we are chiefly indebted for the knowledge that they have treasured up for our use are: 1. Dr William Bennet, formerly Fellow of Emmanuel College, and afterwards Bishop of Cloyne (1790), large extracts from whose manuscript account of the Roman Roads are printed in Lyson's *Magna Britannia*. 2. Dr Charles Mason, formerly Fellow of Trinity College, and Rector of Orwell, who made a trigonometrical survey of the county, and left manuscripts which were used by Gough in his edition of Camden's *Britannia*, and by Lyson in his *Magna Britannia*. 3. We have the very curious,

1

learned, but fanciful works of Stukeley, namely, the *Itinerarium Curiosum*, 1724; and *Medallic History of Carausius*, 1757—1759. 4. Much valuable matter, and many judicious remarks, are to be found in Horsley's *Britannia Romana*, 1732. 5. Dr William Warren, formerly Vice-Master of Trinity Hall, wrote a dissertation upon the subject of the site of the Grantacæster of Bede, which is said to have "demonstrated the thing as amply as a matter of that sort is capable of," that that place is now represented by the Castle End of Cambridge. Brydges informs us that it was the intention of his brother, Dr R. Warren, to publish this tract which came into his hands after the death of the Vice-Master (*Restituta*, iv. 388). It does not appear that he carried out his intention, nor have I succeeded in learning the fate of the manuscript. A note in Gough's *Camden* led me to hope that it might exist in the archives of the *Spalding Gentleman's Society*, but it does not appear that the paper was ever communicated to them, for their minutes, as I learn through the kindness of Mr Charles Green, one of the few members of that ancient and celebrated society, merely record the reading of a letter from the Rev. Mr Pegg, on Sept. 4, 1735, stating the fact of Dr Warren's demonstration, but not giving its mode of proof. As Dr Warren left some manuscripts to Trinity Hall, concerning the antiquities of that college, I had some faint hopes that the missing tract might be preserved amongst them, but the Rev. W. Marsh, now Vice-Master of that society, has had the kindness to examine the papers left by Dr Warren, and informs me that the treatise on Grantacæster is not amongst them.

Having made these preliminary remarks, we proceed to the description of the ancient roads which pass through the county; and, as it will be most convenient to take Cambridge as a starting point from whence to trace those that diverged from it, it will also be proper to occupy ourselves shortly with Cambridge itself.

I. CAMBRIDGE.

THE Roman station of Cambridge was wholly situated to the north of the river Cam, and a considerable part of three of its sides may still be easily traced. If we commence by entering the town from Huntingdon, and immediately turn to the right, we soon find ourselves upon the top of the lofty bank of a broad and deep ditch which was apparently 10 or 12 feet deep, and perhaps nearly 40 in width. Bowtell (MS. ii. 96) says that the width of another part of the ditch was seen in 1802, when men were digging across a spot skirting the east side of the station to obtain brick-earth. The place was called Black-mow Piece, and the ditch appeared to have been 10 to 12 feet deep, and 39 broad. Returning to the bank and passing in front of the Storey's Alms-houses we arrive at the western angle of the ancient town; rounding it, a row of cottages called Mount Pleasant is found to stand upon the top of the rampart, which may be followed through nearly its whole length on that south-western side of the station. Traces of the ditch in front of this face of the fortification could recently be seen, but it is now filled up with rubbish. The lane called Northampton Street, by which an entrance is now obtained into the town from the St Neots road, seems to be carried along the bottom of the rampart, which passing to the south of St Giles's church, defended the south-eastern side in the time of the Romans. Perhaps there was no ditch on this side, and that it was sufficiently defended by the river, a branch of which ran close to it, as we learn from the foundation deeds of St Giles's church, preserved in the Cottonian Library (Gough's *Camden*, 130). The continuation of this river-face of the fortification is well seen in Magdalene College garden, where a terrace-walk is formed upon the vallum. The remaining side towards Chesterton parish is not traceable, having been destroyed in order to form the Norman

1—2

and Cromwellian fortifications of the castle. Half of the north-western side also has been levelled. There appear to have been the usual four gates through which two roads to be presently described passed. The extent was measured by Dr Stukeley, who, however, erroneously includes Pythagoras School within the walls, and found to be "2500 Roman feet from east to west, and 2000 from north to south." Even allowing for the error of including Pythagoras School within the station, it is very difficult to conjecture by what mode Dr Stukeley obtained such a large extent for it. The Roman foot is scarcely $\frac{4}{10}$ of an inch shorter than the English foot, and the real extent of the station (taking the measurements from a recent survey) is about 1650 feet from north to south, and 1600 from east to west, measuring diagonally, as Stukeley seems to have done; or the north-east and south-west sides are each about 1320 feet long, and the north-west and south-east about 930 in length[1].

Bowtell states that some remains of the Roman wall were found in 1804, his words are: "On the interior side of this fosse stood a very ancient wall, some remains whereof were discovered in March 1804, when 'improvements' were making thereabouts by destroying a part of the vallum towards the north-west end, which wall abutted eastwards on the great road near to the turnpike-gate. The materials in the foundation of this wall consisted of flinty pebbles, fragments of Roman bricks, and ragstone so firmly cemented that prodigious labour with the help of pickaxes, &c. was required to separate them. A part of the wall was consequently left undisturbed, and the fosse filled up with earth" (Bowt. MS. ii. 98). He also states that men digging at about the middle of the east side of the station met with the foundations of a stone building, supposed to be part of the Decuman Gate, and that directly opposite across the station similar foundations were seen in 1810 on

[1] On the annexed plan the outline of the station is shown by the broken line.

occasion of the erection of the Lancastrian School (ii. 99).
Mr Bowtell measured one of many Roman bricks found on the
edge of the fosse when the Gaol was built, and states it to
have been 16 inches by 12 inches, and from ⅜ to 1⅜ in thickness (ii. 166). In 1804 at about 100 paces from the north-
west side of the ditch, and to the west of the turnpike-road,
several antiquities were found, such as a cornelian intaglio set
in a finger-ring of silver, and representing Mercury with the
caduceus in his left and a purse in his right hand; also a bronze
figure of Mercury, two inches high, with wings on his bonnet
and feet, and holding a purse (Bowt. MS. ii. 175). Many
Roman coins have been found near to the castle (Gough,
Camden, ii. 219) from an early period; and in 1802 and the
seven following years, 41 of first brass, 25 of second, and 86
of third brass, also 16 of silver, besides others of which 3 were
British were found there (Bowt. MS. ii. 191). A list of the
Emperors, &c. is given below, derived from Vol. VIII. of Bowtell's Collections, in which the coins are all fully described[1].

A second brass coin of Otacilla was found near the castle
in 1846 (*Camb. Antiq. Soc. Cat. of Coins*, 13); a second brass of
Vespasian at the same place and date (l. c. 7); and in 1852
a first brass of Gordianus, and a second brass of Nero. The
coins have chiefly belonged to the later Emperors. Urns,

[1] Coins of first brass of Nero, Trajan, Hadrian, Antoninus Pius,
Marcus Aurelius, Faustina, Commodus, Didius Julianus, Macrinus,
Severus Alexander, Julia Mammæa, Gordianus, Balbinus, Quintus He-
rennius Hostilianus, Julius Philippus.   Of second brass of German-
icus, Claudius, Vespasian, Trajan, Severus Alexander, Faustina, Probus,
Antoninus Pius, Philippus, Gallienus, Carausius, Constantinus Chlorus,
Valerius Severus, Decentius, Theodosius, Constans, Constantinus,
Maximianus, Magnentius, Valerius Licinianus Licinius. Of third brass
of Claudius, Gallienus, Tacitus, Victorinus, Claudius Gothicus, Aure-
lianus, Tetricus, Carausius, Allectus, Fl. Max. Theodora, Carus, He-
lena, Constantinus, Posthumus, Constantius, Crispus, Constantinus
Junior, Constans, Magnentius, Valentinianus, Valens, Theodosius, Gratianus, Arcadius, Honorius. The silver coins were of Trajan, Hadrian,
Faustina, Caracalla, Severus Alexander, Posthumus, Domitian, Gordianus, Otacilla Severa, Philippus.

Pateræ embellished with figures, Querns, Lacrymatories, Armillæ of brass, a variety of Amphoræ and fragments of green and blue glass were found near the castle in 1802—6 (Bowt. ii. 166, 167, 168), and also more recently urns have been found. Stukeley thought that there was a ford at the Great Bridge (*Itin. Cur.* 78). Mr Essex says, that when he was superintending the excavations for the foundation of the Great Bridge in 1754, he saw those of the ancient stone-bridge over the river Graunt, built on piles. It consisted of two small round arches as he learned from finding some of the stones that formed the arch. Mr Essex does not call this bridge Roman but only "very ancient." He says that there was probably a paved ford there in the time of the Romans, which " very plainly shewed itself in the year 1754 as a firm pavement of pebbles." At the same time he states that several pieces of Roman antiquities were found, one of them being a weight, or perhaps the ornament of a standard, which Dr Stukeley called a representation of Carausius's supposed Empress Oriuna (Bowt. v. 944, 945). In Lyson's *Cambridgeshire* (44) Mr Essex is stated to have considered the bridge to be Roman, and that the ford was an idea of Stukeley's. (See also *Reliq. Gal.* 53.)

" A Lachrymatory" was found in removing the foundations of the old Provost's Lodge of King's College. A small Roman vessel was found in the excavation for a sewer in Park Street in 1848. A patera of Samian ware, and a lachrymatory of white clay were found at the south-west corner of Northampton Street in 1847 (C. A. S. Museum). It is stated in Gough's *Camden* that Roman bricks were to be seen in his time in the north-west corner of St Peter's church-wall.

That there was a large station at Cambridge appears, then, to be certain, but the name borne by it in the times of the Romans admits of doubt, and has been discussed at great length by the antiquaries of the last century. I shall only therefore remark that probably it is the CAMBORITUM of the

Itineraries which are peculiarly confused in their reference to this district. That name is given to this station by Gale (*Anton.* 92), where he derives it from " *Cam*, 'fluvius,' *rhyd*, 'vadum'." He is generally believed to be correct, but Stukeley (*Car.* ii. 139) places that station at Chesterford, and Horsley (*Brit. Rom.* 430) at Icklingham. In the same manner DURO-LIPONS has been placed at Godmanchester, which is now generally allowed to be its true site, at Ramsey, and even at Cambridge. Cambridge is the *Caer Graunt* of Nennius (ed. *Gale* 115), for I cannot agree with those who place that "city" at Grantchester where, as I hope to shew, there was only a small fort. Stukeley (*Car.* 160, &c.) invented a city of GRANTA which is unknown to antiquaries, but which he supposed to have been founded by his favourite Emperor Carausius after the compilation of the Itineraries. The name given by Nennius is doubtless a fact in his favour. To conclude, in the words of Bishop Bennet after he had carefully examined the subject, " I feel myself incompetent to affix any certain name to the station at Cambridge, although, if I was obliged to decide, I should on the whole prefer that of CAM-BORITUM."

The position of this fortified town was well chosen, for it is situated on one of the most commanding spots to be found in the district. Its site is the projecting extremity of a low range of hills, backed by a slight depression, or broad and shallow valley. On at least two of its sides the ground fell away rather rapidly from the foot of the ramparts, and the river defended the fourth side. It fronts the only spot where the river could be easily passed by the *Via Devana*, or indeed approached without traversing extensive morasses. Grant-chester possesses none of these advantages, nor is it situated upon either of the great Roman roads.

It is highly probable that the Saxon town of *Grantabrigge* stood upon the same site as the Roman CAMBORITUM, and that it was at a late period, perhaps even after the Norman conquest, that the principal part of the town became stationed on the south side of the river. May not the construction of the Norman castle have been a promoting cause of this removal of the population, as was the case at Lincoln? The Domesday Survey informs us that twenty-seven houses were destroyed for the purpose of building or enlarging the castle of Cambridge, and that what had constituted two of the wards of the town in the time of King Edward the Confessor was then, on account of this destruction of the houses, considered as forming only one ward (*Domesday Book*, i. 189).

Perhaps the very ancient Caer Graunt of the Britons is represented by the village of Grantchester, to which a British trackway will be shewn to have led, and that the Romans, finding it better situated for their purposes, founded CAMBO-RITUM at Cambridge. A similar event seems to have taken place at Norwich, where the present city represents the British town, and Caister the Roman fort in its neighbourhood (see Woodward's *Norwich*). This would remove much of the difficulty which attends the determination of the sites of *Caer Graunt*, *Camboritum*, *Grantacæster* and *Grantebrigge;* indeed all, if Bede is allowed to have been as misinformed concerning the true name of the spot where St Etheldreda's coffin was found as he was of its material (*Caii Hist. Canteb. Acad.* 8.).

It must however be added that the Castle Hill at Cambridge, which is situated within the walls of CAMBORITUM, is manifestly one of the ancient British tumuli, so often found to occupy commanding posts and to have been fortified in after times. The lower part of the hill is natural, but the upper half in all probability artificial. The existence of this tumulus and the want of any ascertained British remains at Grantchester throw doubt upon the above suggestion.

It may be allowable to remark here that the difficulties attending some of the itineraries of Antoninus are very great, owing probably in part to the corruption of the text, but also from the circuitous course taken by them. In that route with which we are interested, viz. the Iter v., it certainly does seem very remarkable that the traveller should be led from London to Colchester on his way to Lincoln; more especially as we find the *Erming Street* forming an almost direct communication between the two places. On examining the Iter vi. we find another route connecting the same stations of LONDINUM and LINDUM, but deviating from the direct course to about as great a distance to the west (to Daventry) as the Iter v. does to the east. This may perhaps be explained by supposing that these itineraries were not meant to give a list of the stopping places upon the great roads of Britain, but are derived from the note-book of some person visiting officially the different stations, and taking such a course as would most conveniently admit of his doing so. Indeed there is only one place of any apparent importance which is situated upon the southern part of the *Erming Street*, and not visited in one or the other of these journeys, viz. AD FINES, which is placed at Braughing in Hert-fordshire. An anonymous writer, who has published *The Ro-man Roads in England*, under the signature " A. H.," suggests with much probability that in Iter v. VILLA FAUSTINA was at Woodbridge and ICIANI at Dunwich, the travellers return-ing from this latter place to Colchester and proceeding along the *Via Devana* to Cambridge, which he names CAMBORITUM. By this scheme the number of miles between the stations accords reasonably well with those stated in the Itineraries, and if the object of the journey was such as I have above sup-posed to be probable, this deviation will not be looked upon as unlikely to have taken place. Mr Neville considers ICIANI to have been at Chesterford, but does not, as far as I am in-formed, explain how he makes that idea accord with the Itine-raries (*Journ. Archæol. Assoc.* iii. 208).

It is worthy of remark that if the usual idea of the Itine-raries forming a kind of road-book, is adopted, we find many undoubtedly Roman roads unnoticed in them. For instance, the *Akeman Street* which passes through Cambridge is omitted, and also that part of the *Via Devana* which lies to the north-west of this town.

II. ANCIENT ROADS THROUGH CAMBRIDGE.

Two great lines of road passed through CAMBORITUM, crossing each other nearly at right angles in the center of the station; namely, (1) The *Akeman Street*, which starting from the north coast of Norfolk terminated by a junction with the *Foss Way* at Cirencester (CORINIUM); and (2) the so-called *Via Devana* leading from Colchester (COLONIA or CAMELODUNUM) to Chester (DEVA); (3) Some fancied roads from Cambridge are noticed after the description of these.

The other roads that passed through any part of the county were (4) the *Erming Street*, (5) the *Icknield Way*, (6) the *Ashwell Street*, (7) the *Peddar Way*, (8) the *Fen Road*, (9) the *Ely and Spalding Way*, (10) the *Suffolk and Sawtry Way*, (11) the *Aldreth Causeway*, (12) the *Bury, Wisbeach, and Spalding Way*, (13) the *Bullock Way*, (14) *Cnut's Dyke*.

1. THE AKEMAN STREET.—(1) *Cambridge to Brancaster.* It left the north-eastern side of the station at CAMBORITUM, not far from the site of the castle, and could be traced over the open fields to King's Hedges as a track for carts, but has recently been obliterated on the inclosure of the parish of Chesterton[1]. I have often walked along it to King's Hedges, where there is a large oblong camp on its southern side, which may be of Roman origin, as Roman coins (particularly one of silver with the head of Roma on one side and Castor and Pollux on horseback on the reverse) have been found there (Gale, *Anton.* 92 ; Gough's *Camden*, ii. 226, from the Aubrey MS.) ; or may have derived its formation from William I., who is believed to have occupied it during his war with the Saxons of the Isle of Ely. Also at a short distance from it on the other side there is a semicircular camp called Arbury, which may have been used by the Romans, as seems to be generally supposed, but from its shape is most probably

[1] Roman vessels have occasionally been found in this parish.

of British origin. In both of these camps the trenches and embankments have been much injured by cultivation and the enclosure of the land. They are both in Chesterton parish, although one side of each of them forms part of its boundary. I do not know of any camp or fort nearer to that village, which is about two miles distant from them. Coins of silver and copper of Trajan, Hadrian, and Faustina have been found at Chesterton, as I learn from Mr E. Litchfield. From King's Hedges the road still exists in the form of a country lane, in some parts presenting the usual raised form of Roman roads, as far as Landbeach; and may then be faintly traced to its junction with the Cambridge and Ely road near Denny Abbey. Soon after passing that place it bore slightly to the right of the present road, and crossed the Old Ouse "at a ford near an Ozier-holt, half a mile below [Stretham] ferry," "having crossed the road and ditch and being visible until it dips into the fen" (Bennet in *Lyson's Camb.* 45); then passing by the east end of Grunty Fen[1] to Ely. From Ely it went to Little-port, where it crossed the Old Ouse river, and the name of which place Stukeley derives from Porth, the Welsh term for a road (*Car.* 143), and where a gold coin of Valerianus has been found; thence to a farm called Cold Harbour, or Coham, as Dr Bennet names it, where he informs us that the road was "visible," and which is situated on the boundary of the county of Cambridge, from which we pass into Norfolk. Here the road seems to have turned to the right in order to cross the Little Ouse river to Southery, in and near to which place Roman vessels have been found and also Roman coins, but mostly in very bad preservation: amongst them were a second

---

[1] In Grunty Fen a gold Armilla, accompanied by several bronze palstaves, was found in 1845 (C. A. S. Museum). At a place called Little Shallows in Burnt Fen, near Prickwillow, which is not far from the line of this road after passing Ely, a bronze vessel resembling a saucepan, with an ornamented flat handle, bearing the maker's name, BODVOGENVS. F., was found in 1838 (*Archœol.* xxviii. 436, t. 25.).

brass of Domitianus, a first brass of Maximinus, a third brass of Constantinus, a small Valentinianus, Urbs Roma, a plated denarius of Postumus, and several others illegible. Again returning to its old direction the road passed Hilgay and Denver, where it was crossed by what I call the *Fen Road*, leading from Peterborough to Swaffham, which will be noticed presently. From Denver it went by Downham and near Lynn to Castle Rising and Brancaster, which was probably the BRANCODUNUM of the Romans.

Although passing through the Fen country, this line of road is so laid down as to take the utmost advantage of the "highlands." It first entered the fen near Denny Abbey, and escaped from it again after crossing the Old Ouse river, a distance of about $1\frac{3}{4}$ mile. It next left the "high-land" at Littleport at the passage of the Ouse, and continued in the fen for about six miles, emerging from it after crossing the Little Ouse to Southery. Between Southery and Hilgay there is less than half a mile of fen, and similarly, there is about half a mile of it bounding the Stoke river, between Hilgay and Fordham on the way to Denver. Thus there was not more than nine miles of fen country to be crossed by the Roman Way between Cambridge and the high ground of Norfolk. We here see a beautiful example of the engineering skill of the Romans. Additional instances will be pointed out in the course of this treatise.

(2) *Cambridge to Cirencester.*—Returning to Cambridge and starting in the opposite direction. The road was, in Bishop Bennet's day, to be " easily followed along the green balks in the fields at the back of the Colleges, until it falls into the common road from Cambridge to Barton at a tumulus." Unfortunately both balks and tumulus have been removed, so that without his help we should have had little more than conjecture to lead us to the belief of its having taken this course. The late Dr F. Thackeray informed me that more than sixty years since he was taken to the point

where the Huntingdon and Barton roads now join, and shewn this line of road extending in both directions as it is here described. It appears to have left the station nearly on the line of a foot-lane called Bandy-Leg Walk, which connects Castle End with the St Neots road, and I have sometimes thought that I could see traces of its ridge in some of the fields between that point and St John's Farm. It joined the present Barton Road at a little beyond Stone Bridge. On arriving at about the third mile-stone from Cambridge it was joined by a road from Grantchester, which will be noticed when describing the *Via Devana*. Then leaving the present turnpike road it passed through Barton churchyard, and, following a farm-track, rejoined the road to Wimpole near Lord's Bridge, at a little beyond which its raised crest is still plainly to be seen near to a tumulus called Hey Hill. This tumulus was opened by Dr E. D. Clarke in 1817, and a skeleton, but no antiquities, was found. Near to the same place a chain with collars for conducting captives, and a double fulcrum to support a spit, both of iron, were found, and are now preserved in the Fitzwilliam Museum, to which they were presented by Dr Clarke. The next year an Amphora covered by a stone, and inclosing a black and two red terra-cotta vases, was found near to Hey Hill (*Archæologia*, xix. 56. t. 4). The Roman track then followed almost exactly the line of the present road. "It leaves Orwell to the left, mounts the range of hills not far from Orwell wind-mill, and descends straight by a hedge-row into a lane," probably the present road "crossing Lord Hardwick's long avenue, and presently after the turnpike-road," which now represents the *Erming Street*, "having Armingford," or, as it is called on the Ordnance Map, Arrington "bridge on the left; it then enters the closes on the opposite side of the road, and seems to have borne to the right towards the Roman station at Sandy" (Lyson's *Camb.* 46). On Orwell hill there is an ancient track-way diverging from it, and keeping on the crest of the hill with a curved course until it joins the

Erming Street at about three miles to the north of Arrington Bridge. It is called the *Mare Way*. Several miles to the north of this track there is a place named Caldecot, and to the north-east of that village, but in the parish of Hardwick, there is an old track-way called the *Port Way*. The three names, as is justly remarked by the Rev. C. H. Hartshorne, are characteristic of spots occupied by the Romans. At about a mile from Hey Hill, and just below the ridge upon which the church of Comberton stands, the remains of a Roman Villa were discovered a few years since in a bed of gravel, for the following account of which I am indebted to the description published by Mr Deck.

VILLA AT COMBERTON.—In February 1842 workmen employed in digging gravel on the low ground between Comberton church and the Bourn Brook, found some massive brickwork, and immediately informed their master of it. He (Mr Wittett) caused the earth to be carefully cleared away and exposed to view the foundations of an extensive Roman building. The plan made by the Rev. J. J. Smith, which is appended to this treatise, will best convey an idea of its form. Each of the piers consisted of 10 tiles, $1\frac{1}{2}$ inches thick, and 8 inches square. The walls were 3 feet thick, and $3\frac{1}{2}$ feet of them was standing. They consisted of masses of Ketton stone, chalk-marl, and immense flints, kinds of stone not found in that neighbourhood. The area was filled with fragments of Roman tiles and bits of coloured stucco and fresco-paintings, of which the colours continued quite bright. Flue tiles still shewed the action of the fire. Fragments of glass and of coarse pottery, also hair-pins formed of the fossil called Belemnite, were found. Coins had for some time past been found at Comberton. On the site in question two of *Septimus Severus* and one of *Gordianus* have been picked up. On one of the square tiles there is a remarkably distinct impression of a wolf's [? dog's] foot, which must have been made when the tile was in the course of manufacture. (Similar marks have been found at Litlington). Also on another there is a perfect impression of a shoe, furnished with nails like those used by country people at the present time. In the village, about 1½ mile to the north of the villa, there is a " Maze" in excellent preservation. (Mr I. Deck in *Camb. Chron.* Mar. 5, 1842.) The spot called the ' Maze' is just in front of the National School, and if it was not known to be ancient might be passed without observation. It is angular in its outline tending to a square, and has from time immemorial been kept paved with pebbles by the villagers. The ditch and bank that once bounded it are now nearly destroyed. Its use and date I am unable to conjecture. There is said to be a similar ' Maze' at Hilton near Fenny Stanton in Huntingdonshire.

In the same newspaper (Oct. 2, 1842) some slight additional information concerning the villa is given. A hexagonal room, with sides ten feet long and walls two feet thick, had been excavated, and many fragments of glass, samian pottery, and fresco painting found in it. This was destroyed before Mr Smith's plan was made. A portion of the leaden pipe and two of the hollow flue tiles through which it passed, two of the tiles (measuring 18 inches by 8) which formed the piers, and two beautiful upper millstones, 19 inches in diameter, are in the Museum of the Cambridge Antiquarian Society. Also in the same collection there will be found a small earthen vessel, resembling the lid of a jar, formed of whitish clay and coated with a red material so as to resemble the samian ware.

Gibson, in his treatise upon Antoninus, expresses an opinion that there probably was a Roman town at Comberton, indeed he hints that the name may be derived from CAMBORITUM, and that place have been there situated. This idea does not seem to be well founded, nor does he place much dependence upon it, as he writes throughout his book as if he was convinced that CAMBORITUM was situated at or close to Cambridge.

To return to the description of the *Akeman Street*. In the

opinion of Mr Hartshorne, with which I concur, the road did not go to Sandy, as was supposed by Dr Bennet, but "passed through Tadlow and Wrestlingworth," by a place called Cold Harbour (a name nearly always associated with Roman or British tracks) and Road Farm, both near to Biggleswade. "On the west side of that town, just below Caldecot Green, it is called Hill Lane, and thence it proceeds to the small circular encampment of Old Warden. In the immediate vicinity we meet with the well-known accompaniments of Roman positions, in Warden Street and Loes Bush" (Hartshorne, *Salop. Antiqua*, 249), and Ickwell Bury. Where it may have led from thence I know not, but another branch of it seems to have gone by Stanford and Stanford Bury to Shefford (where the fine Roman antiquities preserved in the Cambridge Antiquarian Society's Museum were found) and Ampthill, to both which places it is taken by Dr Stukeley.

It seems probable that another track has reached Shefford from the *Erming Street* at Baldock by the way of Norton Bury, Stotfold, Etonbury, and Clifton Bury. Indeed this part of Bedfordshire seems quite full of places of Roman origin.

Beyond Ampthill, Dr Stukeley states that it went by "Rigeway (so called from the road), Woburn, Little Brickhill, Winslow and Edgecot (so called from the road, *agger*); it enters Oxfordshire at Elia Castra, now Alcester, proceeds by Bicester . . . to Stunsfield between Burford and Lechlade to Cirencester" (*Car.* ii. 144). He states that it is called *Akeman Street* in several parts of this course.

There is an *Akerman Street* in Ely, now called Egreman Street. As I learn from the Rev. D. J. Stewart, it is so named in an old survey of Ely, A.D. 1416-17. It does not seem probable that this had anything to do with the *Akeman Street* which, as it probably followed the course of the Littleport Road, must have been crossed by the Akerman Street nearly at right angles.

Concerning a supposed branch of this road Dr Bennet says

that " Dr Mason, who (being rector of Orwell) had many op-
portunities of examining this ground, was of opinion that traces
of another road were to be seen on the south side of the river
near this place [Orwell], which he conceived to have been
thrown off from this in some part of its course, and to have
formed the communication between Cambridge and Verulamium." Of this supposed road nothing more is known.

It must be remarked here that there is another ancient
road also called *Akeman Street*, which appears to have started
from Verulamium and passed by Tring and Aylesbury to Alcester, where it joins the line above described. The application
of the name to this road has been supposed to be an error of
the maker of an old county map, but that seems unlikely from
the name being used, as I am informed, by the country people
about Tring.

2. VIA DEVANA.—(1) *Cambridge to Colchester*. This
road left the Cambridge station by its southern gate, immediately crossing the river close to the site of the present bridge,
where the swampy borders of the river must, from the nature
of the spot, have been narrow.

My friend Mr W. G. Ashton informs me that in the
year 1823 (when he resided in Bridge Street) an excavation
was made for the formation of a great sewer, and that the
late Mr Lestourgeon showed to him a Roman causeway in
very good preservation, extending from near to the Great
Bridge to the church of the Holy Sepulchre, and occupying
about half the width of the street on its eastern side. It
was at about 14 feet below the present surface of the ground,
had black peat earth beneath it, and was covered by a few
feet of the same kind of boggy soil. It was formed of piles
of wood driven into the ground. There were squared beams
of wood (probably oak) placed upon the piles, and thus a
continuous road was formed of such a considerable width
as to allow of its having been used as a way for horses. From
the appearance of the soil, it was supposed to have been

originally elevated a foot, or rather more, above the then surface of the bog, and thus to have formed a dry road to the spot where a Roman bridge is believed to have crossed the river, and of which the remains are said, as has been already remarked, to have been found by Mr Essex (Lysons' *Camb.* 44). The wood was in a good state of preservation, but had become black, as is usual with oak when long buried in a wet peat soil. The fact that it was at least 14 feet below the surface of the present street shows that it must have been of great antiquity; and there being several feet of the peat above it, proves almost conclusively that it had been disused and forgotten before this very ancient part of Cambridge was built. As Grantacæstir is stated by Bede (*Hist.* Lib. iv. c. 19) to have been desolate (civitatulam quandam desolatam) in the seventh century, there may have been sufficient time for the channel of the river to become obstructed at the bridge, and the height of the water being thus raised it would permanently cover the low boggy ground over which this causeway extended. Peat would then quickly form, and in a very few years bury the structure and preserve it for discovery in future ages. There does not seem to be any other period in the history of Cambridge at which these changes could have taken place, without the presence of a population which was interested in the preservation of such a work as that described; and with such an interest it is not credible that the timbers would have been allowed to become totally buried, but would doubtless have been removed, and the whole structure raised so as to admit of its being used, or a different kind of causeway formed to replace that which had become useless.

It may be interesting to remark, before we proceed with the description of the *Via Devana*, that somewhat similar Roman structures of wood have been found in other parts of Britain. In the year 1849, or 1850, a railway was formed along the side of the river Mersey, at Wallasey Pool, near Birkenhead, and in the course of the excavations required in the works for it, a timber bridge was found, covered by 14 feet of silt, and 9½ feet below the present highest level of the tides. As there was a solid bottom in this case, and rocky abutments, piles were not required, and the timbers rested upon the rock and upon two piers of masonry (*Journal of the Architect. Archæolog. and Historic Society of Chester*, Pt. i. 55, and plate). Also, in Lancashire, a wooden causeway, called the Danes' Path, formed of pairs of piles supporting longitudinal timbers, has been traced for a mile and a half across the mosses of Rawcliffe, Stalmine, and Pilling, and is known to have extended for about the same distance further to the ancient sea-beach near Scronka (*Proceedings and Papers of the Historic Society of Lancashire and Cheshire*, iii. 121, and plate). What appear to be conclusive reasons are stated for its being considered as a Roman or Roman-British work. A similar work to that found at Cambridge was discovered in Kincardine Moss, in Scotland, and was undoubtedly a Roman work (Wilson's *Prehist. Annals of Scotland*, 34). Unfortunately, in the case of Cambridge, the attention of antiquaries was not directed to the discovery, and the interesting causeway was either destroyed to give place to the sewer, or again permanently buried under the street at such a depth as to be inaccessible. Although I am myself satisfied, from the above account of the causeway (for which I am indebted to the memory of Mr Ashton of what was shown and explained to him by the late Mr Lestourgeon, who was a gentleman much interested in archæology), it is right to state that Mr E. Litchfield, who also remembers these excavations, does not believe that the piles and timbers which he saw were Roman. For the reasons already stated I am unable to find any other period in the history of Cambridge to which to refer them. It is very unfortunate that the work was not examined by some professed antiquary.

The road nearly followed the course of the modern streets of Cambridge, as far as the church of St Andrew the Great, which Dr Bennet states to be placed upon it. From thence it kept to the left of the present Hills' Road, along the highest part of the land between the fens of Cherry Hinton and Trumpington. Traces of it were probably found in the form of a ridge of gravel, at the distance of three or four yards from that road, when the ground was recently trenched to form a plantation at the border of the Botanic Garden property adjoining the Hills' Road. This is, however, uncertain, as the subsoil of all that district is gravel, and the appearances may have been natural. Traces of it are much more certainly to be found at a little to the east of the Great Tithe Farm, where its ridge may still be seen crossing the private road to the farm, and in the next and one succeeding hedge as you proceed along its course towards the south. These traces, although so very faint, are interesting as confirmatory of Dr Bennet's statement, that it took this course; a statement made before the enclosure and drainage of the lands, and therefore at a time when its ridge was doubtless to be easily observed. We next see it near Red Cross Farm, where it has changed its direction so as to ascend the hills along the course of Worts' Causeway. Its ridge may be observed crossing the private road at a few yards to the north-east of the farm-house in both the neighbouring hedges, and (looking back upon our course) across the whole width of the adjoining field, and in the hedge beyond it; bearing in such a direction as to appear as if its destination was Grantchester, and to which place a road, to be described presently, branched off here. It is probable that the curve in the *Via Devana* and the junction of these two ancient tracks took place at, or very near to, this latter hedge; the line bearing from that point, in one direction straight to CAMBORITUM, and in the other nearly following the present course of the Worts' Causeway in an easterly direction, until it attained the top of the hill, where it regains its original nearly south-east course. The reason for this remarkable deviation from the usual direct line of the Roman roads is to be

found in the formerly impassable character of Hinton Moor,
which would have been encountered if it had been continued
in a straight line to Cambridge. The only mode of reaching
that place, without crossing deep morasses, being the very
course which we have found that it followed, namely, along
the narrow but slightly elevated ridge that separates Hinton
Moor from the marshy track extending from Shelford to the
river Cam, and along which the Vicar's Brook flows, which
supplies the conduits in Cambridge with water. The road
only deviates just sufficiently to avoid the wet country which
near Red Cross extended a little to the west of the Worts'
Causeway.

It was supposed, says Horsley (*Brit. Rom.* 431,) that
a road from Chesterton, which must have crossed the river
near to the present railway bridge, and kept to the east
of Coldham's Common, joined the *Via Devana* at the top of
the hill where we have now arrived ; but no trace of such
a track having, it is believed, ever been observed, it is unnecessary to notice it further.

At this point, where the road returns to its original
direction, there are the remains of two tumuli, called the Twopenny Loaves, one of which was opened in 1778, and seven
skeletons were found at its bottom ; six of them were laid
close together and parallel, with their heads pointing due
north, the other lay with its head directed due west, and
its feet next the side of the nearest of the six (Nichols's
Lit. Anec. viii. 631). At Fulbourn, which lies at a short
distance to the north-east of this point, various British remains
have been found, such as a leaf-shaped sword of bronze,
a spear-head of that metal, and others (*Archæol.* xix. 56, t. 4).
Mr Litchfield has a bronze Roman key found at Fulbourn.

At a short distance to the west of the road near this
point there is a large rudely circular camp, called Vandlebury. It is 246 paces in diameter, has 3 ramparts, and 2
ditches between them (Bowt. MS. vii. 2641), and was pro-

bably a work of the Britons, but is shown, by the discovery of coins, to have been occupied by the Romans. The coins were found in 1685, in digging the foundations of Lord Godolphin's house, which stands within the camp. They were of Valentinian I. and Valens; a knuckle-ring and coins of Trajan and Antoninus Pius were afterwards picked up; in 1730, several large brass coins and a silver ring; and in 1752, a small brass coin of Nero (Gough's *Camden*, ii. 138; *Bibl. Topog. Brit.* iii. xv.; Gale, *Anton*. 93). A coin of Cunobeline has also been found there (Bowtell MS. ii. 96). The hills surrounding this place are now called Gogmagog, which is perhaps a corruption of Hogmagog, itself believed by Gale to have come from "*Hoog macht*, quod *altum robur* significat et naturæ loci satis congruit."

The road is now plainly distinguishable for many miles, with its crest highly raised, and is still used. It crossed the *Icknield Way*, which is represented by the road from Chesterford to Newmarket, at Worsted Lodge passed about a mile to the south of Balsham, a short distance to the north of Horseheath Lodge, and entered Suffolk near Withersfield. In this part it is fully 40 feet wide. Its course from thence to Colchester, by Haverhill and Halsted, it is unnecessary to notice. In Cambridgeshire this part of the Road goes by the name of *Woolstreet*, or Worsted. Near Vandlebury, and between the Woolstreet, and Fleam Dyke, there are many tumuli. At Barham Hall, near Linton, about two miles to the south of the road, there are some very unintelligible intrenchments. They are situated in the first and second fields, beyond the inclosures of the Hall, on the way to Bartlow, between that road and the river Bourn, and have been supposed to be the remains of a camp. There are considerable traces of a scarped slope, but no ditch, upon the north-west and south-west sides of a large space; and near to the entrance of the first field there is a deep trench, which does not seem to have any connexion with the supposed camp.

On the opposite side of the river Bourn and close to it, in
the parish of Hadstock but adjoining the town of Linton, there
was a Roman villa, which was exhumed by the Hon. R. Neville
in 1850, (for an account of it see *Archœol. Journ.* viii. 27).
Gough saw the bronze bust of a satyr found at Linton (Gough's
Camden, ii. 138). In 1832 a boy found a vase containing
many silver Roman coins in a field in the parish of Horseheath,
belonging to S. Batson, Esq. Amongst them there were
those of Nero, Vespasian, Titus, Domitian, Nerva, Trajan,
Hadrian, the two Antonines, Faustina, and L. Ælius Verus.
(*Camb. Chron.*, Oct. 5th, 1832, and Jan. 25th, 1833). At
Bartlow, which is also about two miles from the road, are the
well-known Bartlow Hills, the examination of which attracted
so much attention nearly twenty years since (*Archœol.* xxv. 1,
t. 1—3, and xxvi. 300, t. 31—35). A third brass coin of
Valens was found there (*Archœol.* xxvi. 463). The hills are
formed of a succession of very thin layers of mould and chalk
regularly alternating and horizontal. Mr I. Deck also gave
an account of the opening of one of them, in the *Cambridge
Chronicle* (May 5, 1838), and of another afterwards (*Ibid.*
May 2, 1840).

(2) *Cambridge to Chester.*—Returning to Cambridge and
proceeding in the opposite direction, the *Via Devana* passed
out at the north-western gate of the station, just to the west
of the present junction of the Huntingdon and Histon roads,
and kept almost exactly along the line of the existing turnpike-
road, but "passed through the fields of the farm called How's
House, where a barrow containing several Roman coins was
removed in making the present turnpike-road" (Lysons' *Camb.*
44), by Lolworth hedges and Fen Stanton to Godmanchester,
on its way to Leicester and Chester.

At three miles from Cambridge, on the way to Huntingdon,
a cylindrical stone was found in 1812, which measured 33 inches
long and $12\frac{1}{2}$ in diameter. It was seen by Dr E. D. Clarke,
and bore the inscription IMP . CAES . FLAVI . ConstAN-

TINO . V . LEG . CONSTANTINO . PIO . NOB . CAes.;
also another with LISSIMVS . CAESAR. (*Gent. Mag.* lxxxiii.
Pt. 1. 524, t. 2, f. 6 and 7). At Boxworth, about 8 miles from
Cambridge, a gold coin of Vespasian was found in 1848 (*Camb.
Chron.* Nov. 4, 1848).

(3) *Grantchester and Barton Road.*—It has been already
stated that a road branched off from the *Via Devana* at Red
Cross, and went to Grantchester. Of this we should have
known nothing without the help of Bishop Bennet, who has
given us the following account of it (Lysons' *Camb.* 45). He
says that the *Via Devana* had the appearance of throwing off
a branch to Grantchester, which "seems to descend immediately into Shelford Fen, where it disappears for a short time;
but as the ground rises on the west side of the fen, the road
appears in its old line rising with it; it then crosses the great
London road, just to the north of the village of Trumpington,
goes straight down a green balk in the corn-field opposite,
which soon becomes an old lane leading into Trumpington
Fen, nearly opposite Grantchester church: in the fen it is
again lost, as these ancient roads often are, in low marshy
ground; but on crossing the river and coming again on the
line of the road, it is found keeping its course as before in an
old lane which passes through the village of Grantchester, becomes a more frequented way, leading to Barton, where it falls
into the Roman way from Cambridge," as is stated above.
The bishop adds: "It must not be concealed, however, that
some antiquaries of the present day are not convinced of the
existence of this vicinal way [as a Roman road]; and though
they confess it to have all the marks of a trackway used in
ancient times, are inclined to account for these appearances by
the supposition that when the Roman bridge and causeway
[at Cambridge] were destroyed by the barbarians, travellers
naturally looked on each side of the ruined station for the
nearest fords, and crossed the Cam at Grantchester and Chesterton, as they did the Ouse at Offord and Hemingford; and

as no signs of a raised causeway appear in this line, the idea is by no means destitute of plausibility; of this however any one who traces it may judge for himself." Thus far the bishop. Unfortunately an interval of 50 or 60 years has almost deprived us of the power of judging, by leaving nothing to trace. Between Red Cross and the river at Grantchester all is either destroyed by cultivation or swallowed up in the former fens, now drained and cultivated; during that part of its course, therefore, we must be satisfied with the fact, that in Dr Bennet's days there was manifestly an ancient road passing in that direction. On the Grantchester side of the river it fortunately happens that two fields have not been subjected to the plough, and there the road may still be traced, not however, as stated by Dr Bennet " in an old lane," but proceeding from a ford as a hollowed way in a direct line across the fields to the junction, in the village, of the present roads from Cambridge and Barton, along the latter of which it went nearly but not quite to the end of the village; and then, continuing the same straight course, it proceeded along a bridle-track direct to Barton. As the whole of the latter part of this course is still used as a road, none of the ancient work is to be seen, (indeed in similar soils to that of this part of the county, the ancient tracks are usually found to have lost their original form, and not to differ in appearance from common field roads;) but it is exactly the line described in the above extract. Concurrence is not however equally allowable with that part of the extract which states that the road entered Grantchester by an old lane. That line would be much out of the direct course; and as it is believed that traces of the road itself still exist in one that is truly direct, it may be allowable for us to doubt the correctness of the statement quoted above. The idea also that the course about to be described is the true one, is rendered more probable by the discovery of a square fort adjoining the side of it.

Roman Fort at Grantchester.—This fort is situated at

a distance of about 200 yards from the river, and considerably raised above it so as to command the ford. It is at the southern end of the large field in which the foot-path from Cambridge forks, and the sunken road from it to the river is crossed by the continuation of the path that leads to the church soon after it enters the next field. The fort can never have had much strength, but was doubtless sufficient to protect the detachment which probably was stationed here to defend the only ford that at that time seems likely to have existed for many miles above Cambridge, until assistance could be obtained from that large town not more than three miles distant. Only a small part of the inclosure is observable ; the whole of two of the sides and a portion of each of the others being obliterated by the roads and buildings of the modern village. The north-eastern angle is very distinct, and what is probably the greater part of the north side is well preserved. That side was defended by two ditches with a low flat ridge resembling a raised road between them. There is no bank on the outer side, but the outer ditch is now about 3 feet deep ; the central ridge then rises a little more than one foot, and is 11 feet broad ; then succeeds the other ditch, on the inner side of which the bank is 4 feet high, thus raising the rampart about a foot above the general level of the field. The whole width of this system of ditches is 40 feet, and the existing length of this side of the fort is 324 feet.

The eastern side remains tolerably perfect to the extent of 189 feet, and was defended by a ditch of about 4 feet in depth, but of which the width cannot be ascertained owing to the presence of a hedge and bank. At a distance of 187 feet from this eastern side, and parallel to it, there are faint traces of a road or street crossing the station, and slightly sunk below the general level. It communicates with the northern boundary ditch, and is probably the road so commonly found to pass through the center of a Roman camp ; of the other which generally crosses it at right angles there is no trace. If this idea is correct, we may conjecture that the camp was 125 yards long. Of its breath we have no such means of judging, but it appears to be probable, from the nature of the ground, that it was about 75 yards. See Plan, Plate 3.

It may be justly asked, how do you know that this was a Roman fort? To which it can only be answered, that there is nothing more than great probability in favour of that opinion; and that it greatly resembles other forts constructed by that people. I am glad to be able to strengthen my own opinion on the matter by adding that of my friend Mr A. Taylor, an antiquary whose attention has been especially directed to the roads and stations of the Romans in Britain, and whom I had the pleasure of conducting to Grantchester in search of a Roman station and road. He remarked upon seeing these banks, which I had previously known but not understood, that it was undoubtedly a Roman work.

To return to the road. In the extract from Dr Bennet's sketch given above, the road to this fort from Red Cross has been traced to the banks of the river, and it is also stated that it did not follow the course from that point laid down by him until it reached the middle of the village at the junction of the Cambridge and Barton roads. As the north-western angle of the fort was situated almost exactly at the junction of the above-mentioned modern roads, and the track from thence to Barton has been already described; we may now turn back from that point and connect it with the Bishop's line at the river. It is certainly curious to find that this well-preserved part of the road is not elevated as is usual with Roman roads, but appears as a slight trench continuing nearly but not quite in a straight line the trenches which form the northern side of the fort. It may be very clearly traced through the 200 yards' interval between the fort and the river, to which it attains by a gradual slope formed by a rather deep cutting in the somewhat abrupt bank overhanging the stream. On the opposite side of the river, in Trumpington Fen, there is a gap in the bank forming a gradual descent to the water, which is now used by cattle as a watering-place, and is the only break in that abrupt bank for a very considerable distance. Shall I be considered as too bold if I state my strong suspicion that it is a trace of the ancient ford? The modern embankment further back from the stream has effectually obliterated the road almost as soon as it attained the level of the adjoining land. I cannot pretend to account for the fact of this road appearing as a trench, but it may be remarked, that British roads are often, perhaps always, sunk below the general level of the country, and have usually a slight bank on each side; and that this road may have been found in existence by the Romans and, as being a track of very little consequence after the foundation of CAMBORITUM, may have been left by them in its original state, but the small fort thrown up as a habitation for the detachment placed there to command the ford. Roman coins have occasionally been found at Grantchester, but I have seen only two of them belonging to the Emperors Valentinianus and Constantinus Junior[1].

At a place where gravel was formerly obtained in the parish of Trumpington, but situated at about a quarter of a mile back from the bridge over Vicar's Brook on the road from Cambridge, many Roman urns have been found in what appears to have been an extensive cemetery. It is recorded in Dr Warren's MSS. now in the possession of Trinity Hall, that about the year 1711 several pateræ, urns, &c. were found in digging gravel at that place. The potter's marks on the pateræ were, OF . LICINI ., OF . MRRAI ., MASCLERVS ., and DAMONI. (Bowt. MS. ii. 179). A coin of Trajan has been found there (*Ibid.* 189). Dr Mason records (Gough's *Camden*, ii. 131) the discovery of many curious pateræ of fine red earth : one large vase three feet long, brass lagenæ, a brass dish embossed, the handle of a sacrificial knife, the brasses of a pugillaris or table-book, some large bones and Roman coins.

---

[1] Grantchester bore the name Grantesete at an early period.

They are preserved in the Library of Trinity College. Dr
Stukeley had in 1751 a Roman cup and saucer entire of fine
red earth, which were dug up at Trumpington (Weld's *Hist. of
Royal Soc.* i. 527). Three urns of rude workmanship found
in that parish, and which were formerly in the possession of
the Rev. J. Hailstone, late vicar, are in the Cambridge Antiquarian Society's Museum.

The late Mr Alex. Watford, who was employed, as he
stated to the Rev. J. J. Smith, to survey at least four-fifths of
the parishes near Cambridge, considered that there was a road
which would continue this track from Barton by Toft to join
the *Erming Street* at Bourn. This would pass by Comberton
church, and therefore just above the Roman villa already
mentioned, by Toft church, near which remains were found
at a place called Priory Field, not far from the brook, in
December 1851, by some labourers digging gravel. At about
three feet below the surface they found seven skeletons. Six of
the bodies had been placed side by side with their feet towards
the west, and the seventh lay across their legs. Fragments of
"Roman pottery, a portion of a lamp and pateræ" were found
close by the skeletons (*Camb. Chron.* Dec. 27, 1851). An
instance of a nearly similar arrangement of seven bodies has
been already mentioned. Then this supposed road would pass
by a place called Kingston Stones to Bourn, where two urns
called Roman, and half a quern formed of pudding-stone, were
found in 1813 (*Archæol.* xviii. 435). It is there stated that
no trace of a Roman road or station was known to be near to
them, and if there was a road following this course, as is not
improbable, it most likely was of British origin.

3. OTHER SUPPOSED ROADS FROM CAMBRIDGE.—Having
concluded the account of the two great lines of communication
passing through Cambridge, I might proceed at once to describe the others which are intended to form part of this
treatise; but it is desirable first to mention two other lines
which have been supposed to have started from that town.

(1) *Cambridge to Chesterford.*—Dr Bennet states his belief that there was a road from Cambridge to Chesterford, proceeding nearly on the line of the present turnpike-road by Great Shelford and Sawston, but no trace of it has been observed. At Shelford, and therefore close by the side of this supposed road, there is a fine rectangular camp at a spot now called Granham's Farm. It is 350 yards long from east to west, and rather more than 100 from north to south. The bank is very lofty and perfect throughout its eastern half, but has been levelled in the other part, owing to the house and farm premises being within the camp. The ditch, of great breadth, may be traced throughout a much greater portion of its extent, and is wet, part being now choked with bog and part full of water.

On the top of Huckeridge Hill, near Sawston, some men removing gravel in Aug. 1816, found a skeleton at 3 feet below the surface. At the feet of the skeleton there were placed two vessels of bronze, the larger 15 inches across, and having a flat rim ornamented with a row of bosses all round. They found also some black coarse earthenware; an iron sword 2 ft. 7½ in. long; the iron umbo of a shield; and a bronze fibula formed like a double-headed snake. The remains were purchased by Dr E. D. Clarke for the University (*Archœol.* xviii. 340. t. 24 and 25). It is probable that they are Saxon or Danish remains.

(2) *Cambridge to Braughing.*—Dr Stukeley mentions another road leading from Cambridge to Braughing, the AD FINES of the Romans, where it fell into the *Erming Street.* He says that he "could discern many traces of it in the present road, as particularly beyond Barley," and he observed "several milestones, particularly a little on this side Harestreet." Dr Bennet takes no notice of this line, although he quotes Stukeley's *Medallic History of Carausius,* from which (ii. 144) the above extract is taken. I think that the real road to AD FINES commenced at Chesterford passing by Strethall, Little-

bury Green, also called Stretley, Leebury, Pond Street, and then through a country with which I am totally unacquainted, to Hare Street and Braughing.

III. OTHER ANCIENT ROADS IN CAMBRIDGE-SHIRE.

4. THE ERMING STREET.—Nearly the whole of the course of this road through Cambridgeshire is exactly occupied by a turnpike-road. Starting from London and passing Cheshunt and Ware it reached Braughing (AD FINES); it proceeded by Buntingford and Royston, following the line of the present road to Godmanchester (DUROLIPONS). At Braughing it threw off, as I suppose, the road already mentioned to Chesterford. At Royston it crossed the *Icknield Way*, and at two miles further north the *Ashwell Street*. At Arrington Bridge the *Akeman Street* was crossed by it. At about three miles from Godmanchester it passes a spot called Latenbury. It went through the middle of the station DUROLIPONS, the *Via Devana* appearing to have passed on the outside of it on the north-east, and the Roman road from Sandy similarly on the west[1]: the three combined to cross the river Ouse together. From God-manchester its course was by Alconbury Hill, Sawtry, and Stilton (a little to the west of which place there is a Caldecot at about midway between the *Erming Street* and the *Bullock Road*) to Chesterton on the Nen, and Castor, the sites of DUROBRIVÆ of Antoninus and DURNOMAGUS of Richard of Cirencester, to Lincoln. Between Alconbury Hill and Sawtry this is now called *Stangate*. Gale supposed that it crossed the Ouse at Offord (or Oldford) a little above Huntingdon, near a spot called Port Mead; but that does not seem to have been the

---

[1] DUROLIPONS appears to have been hexagonal and placed in the angle formed by those two roads, but traversed by the greater and probably more ancient way now called the *Erming Street*. The outline of the station may probably be traced in the lanes surrounding the modern town.

case with the Roman road, although the original British *Erming Way* may have passed there, having come from Sandy by Eynesbury; I am, however, more inclined to think that it passed the river at or very near to Eynesbury; but of this mention will be made under the head of *Bullock Road*. Horsley, who will not allow that there was any station at Huntingdon or Godmanchester, adopts Gale's idea, and says of this line coming from the north, that "where it is last visible on the south side of the river [Nen], it falls obliquely on to the present post-road, and so has probably crossed it near Chesterton" (Horsley, *Brit. Rom.* 431). He is apparently in error when, speaking of the oblique direction of its junction with the post-road, he states that that shows it to have crossed that road. If we may trust to the Ordnance Map, as I believe to be the case, the road is quite straight for about ten miles, or for five on each side of DUROBRIVÆ, the station close to Chesterton; and it is the turnpike-road that joins it at an acute angle, and changes its original direction for that of the Roman line. It is probable that the British (or other early) way coming from Lincoln, and now called *King Street*, after passing through Castor (DURNOMAGUS), crossed the river with the *Erming Street*, and accompanied it through DUROBRIVÆ, but then turning to the right parted from it and passing along the "convenient ridge of high ground" mentioned by Horsley, became what is now called the *Bullock Road*, of which a description is given in a future page.

Gibson (*Anton.* 142) considers that DUROBRIVÆ was a name applied to the camps placed on both sides of the river Nen at Castor, Alwalton, Chesterton, and Water Newton, at all of which places he states that remains of them have been found. He states that the name means "camps by the river," or the "water-cities." In the *Itinerary* of Richard of Cirencester (a work deserving of little confidence owing to its more than doubtful authenticity) we find DURNOMAGUS in the place that is occupied by DUROBRIVÆ in Antoninus; and it is supposed that the former was that part of the town which was situated on the northern side of the river at and about Castor, and the latter the part lying to the south of the river between Chesterton and Water Newton. Gibson's work above quoted contains an account of DUROBRIVÆ as it was then (1769) known, and Mr Artis has recently made very extensive excavations at Castor, and published a series of plates illustrative of his discoveries[1]. A list of Roman coins found at Castor is given in the Journal of the Archæological Association (ii. 265). A short statement of some of Mr Artis's discoveries is also in that Journal (i. 1), and in the *Gentleman's Magazine* (xci. Pt. 1. 483), it is stated, that the antiquities were distributed over a spot of a triangular shape, of which two of the sides are 2 miles, and the other side 1½ mile in length, the churchyard of Castor being at the apex. Supposing the triangle to stand north and south, as is most probable, this space would include nearly, if not quite, all the places mentioned by Gibson.

5. THE ICKNIELD WAY.—It may easily be traced from near Thetford by Icklingham, where there are Roman remains, and where Horsley placed the ancient CAMBORITUM, crossing the river Lart at Lackford, and falling into the line of the present turnpike-road at Kentford; it forms from thence the boundary of the counties of Suffolk and Cambridge as far as a point upon Newmarket Heath, about half a mile to the north-east of the *Devil's Ditch*. At a little distance to the east of Newmarket it passes a tumulus called Bury Hill. We are told by Dr Bennet—for I believe that its exact course is at present unknown—that "keeping to the hilly ground to the east of the present road, it bears directly for Ickleton, without bending out of its course or inclining towards the considerable Roman station at Chesterford, not far from which it passes. It is remarked by Stukeley and Mason that, in its crossing one of the ancient ditches," the *Brent* or *Pampisford Ditch* (Gough's *Camden*, 141), "so common in this part of the country, the

---

[1] I have not succeeded in obtaining access to a copy of this work.

fosse has been evidently filled up to admit the road." It appears almost certain from this remark, that those antiquaries, or Mason alone (for he is the person mentioned by Gough), traced some part of its course in our county. We are informed above that it kept to the east of the present road from Newmarket to Chesterford, and I had hoped that the boundaries of parishes might restore its probable line. These boundaries do not however much assist us. They are very irregular in the neighbourhood of the present road throughout the northern half of the debated district, except that they coincide with it between Bangalore Barn and the Green Man; from the *Balsham Dyke* to the point where it becomes the boundary of the county they exactly follow its course. In all probability, then, this latter part of the modern road is on the line of the ancient one. When within less than a mile of Great Chesterford it makes a turn nearly at right angles with its former course to pass Ickleton, the county boundary accompanying it round the curve. It then probably went by Ickleton Grange to a point near Chrishall Grange, from whence it may be traced as a nearly disused track to Known's Folly, near to which spot it becomes the boundary of the counties of Cambridge and Hertford. It may be followed by Royston and Baldock, and so to Dunstable. Dr Bennet found it to be "very manifest on the hill-side south-west of Ickleton and on the Downs near Royston." There is no trace of it now in the former place, which is ploughed up, but it is used as a road near the latter. Near to this road Mr R. C. Neville found, in the year 1847, at a place called Five Barrow Field (which is about one mile and a half from Royston, two from Melbourn, and three from Barkway), cinerary vessels of unbaked clay and a coin of the first brass of Marcus Aurelius; also a covered way extending from S.E. to N.W. At two miles distance, he informs us, that there is another similar way extending as far as the eye can reach to the westward. (*Archæologia*, xxxii. 357. *Sepult. Explor.* 25).

Mr Woodward supposed that the *Icknield Way* starting from Norwich passed by Buckenham to Ixworth, and from thence to Bury St Edmund's. In my opinion, and in that of the Ordnance Surveyors, it may still be traced from near Thetford to Kentford. Mr Woodward lays down a British way on the line which I believe to have been taken by the *Icknield Way*, viz. from Norwich by Wymondham and Attleborough to Thetford. (*Archœol.* xxiii. 368).

6. ASHWELL STREET.—This name is now employed to designate a straight piece of road extending from near Ashwell to the *Erming Street* near Kneesworth. It was supposed to be the *Icknield Way* by the Rev. Dr Webb, Master of Clare Hall and Rector of Litlington, and is called Roman by him. In the former idea I believe that he will be generally considered to have then been in error, in the latter he is most probably correct. This road seems to have commenced at Shefford, passed by Etonbury, Stotfold, and Newnham (a little to the south of Caldecot), by Harborough Banks, which is " a camp of 12 acres, where coins, &c. have been found" (Sharpe's *Gaz.* i. 78). Within a mile to the east of Ashwell it enters Cambridgeshire, and passing at about a mile to the south of Litlington church, and crossing the *Erming Street*, was continued to Melbourn Bury. From that place it seems to have passed between the southern point of the deep morass called Melbourn Common, and the northern end of the *Bran* (or as I call it for distinction sake, the *Haydon*) *Ditch*, to Foulmire, Triplow, a little to the south of Whittlesford, where it crossed the southern branch of the river Cam, through Pampisford, by the northern end of the Brent Ditch to join the *Icknield Way* and *Peddar Way* at Bourn Bridge.

Between Caldecot and Henxwell were found, in 1720, many urns, with bones and ashes, several skeletons lying to the south-east, some pateræ with names, lachrymatories, fibulæ, beads, &c.; also in 1724, three pateræ, two patellæ of red earth, an ampulla, a small urn of different colours, a glass lachrymatory, the handle and neck of a glass simpulum, stone handle of a sword, brass fibulæ, &c., were found in Henxwell parish. (Minutes of Soc. of Antiq. quoted in Gough's *Camden*, i. 342).

LITLINGTON.—An account of the Roman burial-place by the *Ashwell Street*, "the line of communication between the Roman station at Ashwell and that at Chesterford," is given in the *Cambridge Chronicle* (April 26 and May 17, 1821). It is stated that 80 urns containing human bones, between 20 and 30 simpula, 20 pateræ of the red samian ware, 20 lachrymatories, and about 30 earthen vessels were found. Also 2 urns of green glass, one square with each side measuring 8 inches and the height 13 inches, the other smaller; the handles of both are massive and beautiful, very similar to those described in the *Archæologia* (Vol. x. and xiv.), as discovered at Lincoln and Haverhill. Also two glass vessels with long necks and straight handles. The pateræ of samian ware have the potter's marks PATER. F., GRACISSA . F., ELVILLI., DIVI-CATVS., &c.; they are 6 or 7 inches in diameter; some have a leaf on the edge but no potter's mark. They frequently served as covers to the urns. An urn, a simpulum, and a patera were in general found together; the simpulum contiguous to the urn; the patera, if not used as a cover, placed perpendicularly touching the urn. Many tiles were found of about three-fourths of an inch in thickness, 17 inches in length, and 12 in breadth, and somewhat concave, and turned down at the edges about an inch. Coins were found of Constantine (silver), having on the reverse three stars over a globe placed upon an altar, with VOTIS over it and XX beneath, surrounded by the motto BEATA TRANQUILITAS; one of Antoninus Pius, of Alexander Severus and Quintilius[1].

To these Dr Webb adds (*Archæol.* xxvi.) coins of Hadrian, Quintilius, Carausius, and Magnentius; also a Roman style of brass, and a number of fibulæ of brass. Several Saxon coins, being silver pennies of Burgred of Mercia and of

[1] Some of the sepulchral vessels are figured in Smith's *Collect. Antiqua.* i. t. 12.

Ethelred the Elder, have been found (*Camb. Chron.* May 17, 1821). Many of these antiquities are now preserved at Clare Hall.

At a meeting of the Cambridge Antiquarian Society (May 6, 1841), the late Rev. W. Clack exhibited coloured drawings of a tesselated pavement found in a Roman villa at Litlington (*Camb. Chron.* May 8, 1841), and at another meeting (Dec. 6, 1841) he gave an account of his whole proceedings in the exploration of the villa, which consisted of more than thirty rooms and a bath (*Camb. Chron.* Dec. 11, 1841). It was situated between the *Ashwell Street* and Litlington church, and the examination of it was mostly made in the year 1829 (*Camb. Chron.* May 29, 1829). Unfortunately Mr Clack's collections were sold in Devonshire, and cannot now be traced.

At Limlow or Limbury Hill (marked as " Tumulus" only on the Ordnance Map), which is about half a mile to the south of the above burial-place, skeletons, with coins of Claudius, Vespasian, and Faustina were found in 1833, as we learn from the communications of the Rev. Dr Webb, made to the Society of Antiquaries, and published in the *Archæologia* (xxvi. 368. t. 44 and 45, also page 374).

The Society of Antiquaries has a large olla of Anglo-Roman ware, much broken, found in 1843 at Melbourn, and presented to the Society by Mr Alex. Watford of Cambridge. It is 12½ inches high, and 7½ inches wide at the mouth (Way's *Cat. of Antiq. &c.* 17).

The Chronicle Hills, three tumuli, which stood in a line bearing north and south upon the eastern side of a brook which divides the parishes of Triplow and Whittlesford, and a short distance to the north of the supposed continuation of the *Ashwell Street*, were levelled in 1819. They contained the remains of skeletons. Adjoining them an ancient well was found filled with broken pieces of pottery with red and black glazing, and a number of tiles formed to overlap each other. Remains of interments were also found in other tumuli near the Chronicle Hills, and the remnants of a bronze vessel. One of the skeletons was in a sitting posture. In both of these cases bones of animals were observed, and especially an enormous quantity of very small bones, but the animal to which they belonged was not determined (*Gent. Mag.* lxxxix. 1. t. 27; *Camb. Chron.* No. 13. 1819).

Near Foxton, which lies to the north of Foulmire, an Amphora, a much broken vase of Arretine ware, and other articles of Roman pottery, were found in 1852 (*Camb. Antiq. Soc.* Comm. i. 43. pl.), also a Roman key of bronze.

At Hinxton and Whittlesford coins of the earlier emperors have been picked up, as I am informed by Mr E. Litchfield.

7. PEDDAR WAY.—The Rev. C. H. Hartshorne (*Salopia Antiqua*, 274) has employed this term to designate an ancient, probably Roman, road, which, having no recognized name throughout the greater part of its course, bears this appellation in the part which lies between Castle Acre and the sea. It began at Stratford-le-Bow near London, and passing Woodford, Epping, Harlow, Bishop's Stortford, and Newport, reached Great Chesterford, at about a mile beyond which it joined the *Icknield Way*, and they proceeded together at least as far as Worsted Lodge on the *Via Devana*, and perhaps to Mutlow Hill Gap in the *Balsham Dyke*. It is probable that they separated at the former place, and that the *Peddar Way* went by Shardlow's Well at the northern end of the stronger part of the *Balsham Dyke*, and then along a series of lanes commencing a little to the south of Great Wilbraham, and extending to the Beacon tumuli at Upper Hare Park on the ascent of Newmarket Heath. These lanes are now called the *Street Way*, and it is by the side of them that Mr Neville has recently excavated an extensive Anglo-Saxon burial-place, and found many valuable antiquities[1]. It seems then to have passed through what is now called the Running Gap in the *Devil's Ditch*, by the end of the marshy ground at St Mindred's

---

[1] See "Saxon Obsequies illustrated by ornaments and weapons discovered by the Hon. R. C. Neville in a cemetery near Little Wilbraham, 1852."

Well, otherwise called Favin's Head, to Exning, where many
Saxon and Roman (*Camb. Antiq. Soc.* Rep. vi. 10, and Museum)
remains have been found. From Exning its line lay apparently
by Chippenham and Badlingham to Mildenhall (where Roman
remains have been found, as I learn from Mr Arthur Taylor),
or Barton Mills, by Mareway or Portway Hill (by both of
which names the place is known) to Brandon, and so by
Mundford, Ickborough, and Hilborough, to Swaffham and
Castle Acre, terminating at Brancaster. According to this
view of the course of the *Peddar Way*, it would appear to
have supplied the place for the Romans of the older British
Icknield Way throughout that part of its course which lies to
the east of Chesterford. The *Ashwell Street* probably did the
same for many miles to the west of that place. The late
Mr Woodward supposed that the *Peddar Way* reached Castle
Acre from quite a different district. He brings it in a direct
line from Ixworth in Suffolk by Brettenham, leaving Swaffham
a little to the west (*Archæol.* xxiii. 370. t. 31). It is stated
by him that the road is tolerably distinct from Brettenham to
the west side of Merton Hall near Watton.

Mr R. Gale states (*Rel. Gal.* in *Bibl. Topog. Brit.* iii. 117),
that at a place called by the country people Starbury Hill,
just above the London road by Audley End, there are the
visible remains of a square work, where the author of Sir Thos.
Smith's life (p. 130) tells us Roman money has been found,
particularly a golden coin of Claudius; which is also confirmed
by Hollinshed (p. 218), who mentions likewise the finding of a
great antique silver cup there. This camp is stated to be
square, but is probably what is now called Ring Hill, although
certainly that intrenchment is not square.

The Hon. R. C. Neville has examined the Roman station
at Chesterford with great care, and collected a very extensive
Museum of the remains disinterred there under his directions,
which is preserved at Audley End. He considers Chesterford
to have been the ICEANUM of the Romans. He has given an

account of these antiquities in two privately printed volumes entitled, *Antiqua explorata*, and *Sepulta explorata*, and also a sketch of his proceedings in the *Journal of the Archæological Association* (iii. 208 and 344).

The same antiquary has made excavations at Mutlow Hill, a large tumulus close adjoining the Balsham Dyke. He found Roman remains consisting of bronze fibulæ, armillæ, &c., and 79 coins, including those of Antoninus Pius (silver); Domitian, Trajan, Hadrian, Aurelius, Commodus, and Caracalla, of first brass; Vespatian, Titus, Hadrian, Antoninus Pius, Lucius Verus, of second brass; Constantine, Licinius, Gratian, Victorinus, Postumus, Allectus, Claudius Gothicus, Tetricus, Valentinian, of third brass. These were found in the examination of the foundations, composed of large bricks shaped from chalk, of a circular building, measuring 35 feet across, and with three feet thickness of wall (*Archæol. Journ.* ix. 229).

Two of the barrows on the edge of Newmarket Heath, belonging to the group called the Beacons, were examined in May 1846 by a party from Cambridge. In one of them nothing was found, as it appeared to have been previously opened; in the other the remains of a British interment, consisting of a rude vase (now in the Cambridge Antiquarian Museum), a few bones, and some ashes, were discovered. (*Camb. Chron.* May 23, 1846).

In removing a barrow for the purpose of improving the exercise ground on Newmarket Heath, an urn of rude construction and materials, containing ashes and some bones, was found in its centre; also two coins, supposed to be Roman, and a fragment of a cup of far superior manufacture to the urn above mentioned, were found lying amongst the soil at the depth of about two feet (*Camb. Chron.* Jan. 26, 1827).

Several Roman antiquities have been found at Exning, of which two urns are in the Cambridge Antiquarian Museum; and many coins of the later Roman Emperors have occurred there, but they are mostly illegible.

There appears to have been a road leaving the *Peddar Way* at Bishop's Stortford, crossing the *Erming Street* at Braughing, and continued to Baldock; passing by a track already noticed to Shefford, and perhaps carried on by Bedford, Higham Ferrars, Kettering, and Market Harborough to Leicester. This cross track probably started from Colchester, passing Braintree and Dunmow on its way to Bishop's Stortford.

8. THE FEN ROAD.—This road appears to have started from the coast of Norfolk at Happisburgh, passed by Walsham, Reepham, and Swaffham, where it crossed the *Peddar Way* to Denver near Downham Market, where it also crossed the *Akeman Street*, and proceeded in a pretty direct line to the high land at Norwood Common at about a mile to the north of March, near to which (on the road to Wisbech, and therefore probably not far from the line of the Roman Way) three urns full of burned bones, and a pot containing 160 denarii of nearly all the Emperors from Vespasian to Antoninus Pius inclusive, were found in 1730 (Gough's *Camden*, 141*); an aureus of Valentinianus was found there in 1845; then by a place called Edernell to Whittlesey, and the neighbourhood of Standground. It perhaps crossed the river at Peterborough, from whence Dr Bennet states that it had, in his time, been recently traced to the Roman station near Castor, and Mr Gibson says positively that that was its course; passing from Peterborough in a straight line through Milton Park, and the then open field to Love Hill, and so on to the center of the camps at Castor (*Antoninus*, iii.); or it may have gone direct to Chesterton, and joined the *Erming Street* before crossing the river. Sir W. Dugdale, in his *History of Embanking*, (p. 175) speaks of this road as follows: "Neither is the long causeway made of gravel of about 3 feet in thickness and 60 feet broad (now [1662] covered with moor, in some places 3, and in some others 5 feet thick), which extendeth itself from Downham in Norfolk (near Salter's Lode) over the great wash to Charke; thence to March, Plantwater, and Edernell,

and so to Peterborough, in length about 24 miles, likely to
be other than Roman work, as may be seen from the words
of Herodian (Lib. 3) in the life of Severus the Emperor,
where taking notice how hardy and warlike a people the
Britons were, and of their expertness in swimming, he saith:
' Sed imprimis tamen curæ habuit pontibus occupare paludes,
ut stare in tuto milites . . . . siquidem pleraque loca frequentibus
oceani alluvionibus paludescunt; per eas igitur paludes barbari
ipsi natant.' " In another place he remarks: " Mr Jonas
Moore (the chief surveyor of this great work of draining in
Cambridgeshire and the counties adjacent) tells me that the
causeway I formerly mentioned is 60 feet broad in all places
where they have cut through it, and about 18 inches thickness
of gravel lying upon moor, and now in many places 3 feet
deep under a new accession of moor" (Sir W. Dugdale to
Sir T. Brown 1658, in *Brown's Posth. Works*, p. 4). Stukeley
says that it was often discovered when digging the drains.
I know nothing personally of this line. The difficulty of
tracing an ancient road through such a country is of course
peculiarly great; as however the Ordance Surveyors mark a
line throughout the whole of the above course from Denver
Sluice to Whittlesey it is nearly certain that they saw traces
of it. On the line of this road we find that there are eleven
miles of fen between Denver and March, and four between
the latter place and Eldernet, and 1½ mile from Whittlesey
to Horsey Hill, where the road crossed the Old Nen river.

In the course of the formation of the Railway at March
three Roman vases were found in a bed of gravel three feet
below the surface at Norwood Side by March, which are now
in the Wisbech Museum. " In 1730, when the road was
making from Wisbech to March [between March common
and Guyhirne], two urns were found, in one of which were
bones and ashes, and in the other about 300 pieces of silver
coin, of all the Roman Emperors from Vespasian to Constantius, both inclusive, no two pieces alike (*Reliq. Gal.* in *Bibl.*

Topog. Brit. iii. 163, and 465, where they are described). Also a few years since [before 1827] some coins of Adrian were found in a field of Mr Richards'; and more recently, in digging a hole for a gate-post, nearly half a peck of base silver, of about the time of Gallienus, was found at Stoney, near March" (Watson's *Wisbech*, 588).

A large quantity of Roman pottery, including samian ware and sepulchral urns, was presented to the Wisbech Museum, in Jan. 1848, by Mr W. E. Rose, which had been found at Stoney in the course of the formation of the railway at that place (*Camb. Chron.* Jan. 8, 1848).

Mr I. Deck possesses a necklace of 46 rough amber, and three blue glass "druidical" beads, found with a bronze spear-head and various other "Roman" implements. They were found in company with a skeleton in Maney Fen, and were probably British rather than Roman (*Camb. Chron.* May 2, 1840). Maney is at some distance from any of the old roads, and in the heart of the fens.

At Thorney, which is a few miles to the north of Whittlesey, many urns and coins very well preserved have been dug up near to the church. There were several coins of Trajan (Watson's *Wisbech*, 560).

About the year 1742, several Roman lamps were found by a man who was ploughing at Glassmore (a district belonging to Whittlesey); they were made of red ware, and all found lying very regularly in a row (Watson's *Wisbech*, 569. Minutes of Spald. Soc. in Gough's *Camden*, ii. 140*).

Mr Woodward supposed that this road reached Denver by a direct route from Norwich, passing by Ovington and Oxburgh. He mentions that traces of a road have been noticed at Hetherset, on a farm called Plainard's,—also in the parish of Saham, where three Roman pigs of lead were found,—likewise that there is a Roman encampment at Ovington,—and that Roman coins have been found at Oxburgh (*Archæol.* xxiii. 368). This is an extremely likely course for a road to have taken;

but, even allowing of its existence, it does not destroy the high probability of the line by Swaffham having also existed. There appear to be traces of an ancient road passing by Stradset to Swaffham, and also, I think, to the east of that place on the way to Happisburgh, and perhaps Norwich.

9. ELY TO SPALDING.—Dr Stukeley believed that a road branched from the *Akeman Street* at Littleport (at least so I understand his remarks), and went by the way of Welney, probably along the line of the Old Causeway Dyke to Upwell and Elm ; and from thence in a direct line to Spalding. It seems to have kept on the western side of the Ouse (which then ran in the course of what is now called the Welney River) to Welney, at which place many Roman coins have been found (Gough's *Camden*, 141*), of which Watson (*Wisbech*, 553) tells us that they were obtained in 1718 (Cole's MS.), and that plates of them were engraved and presented to Trinity College Library by Beauprè Bell. At Upwell it probably crossed the river and took a direct course along the Old Causeway Dyke to Upwell, near to which place, in 1844, "some labourers digging upon an old Roman road, in the occupation of G. Wooll, Esq. ... found two vases filled with coins of various sizes in an excellent state of preservation" (*Gent. Mag.* N. S. ix. 302). The road appears to have again crossed the river immediately after passing Upwell.

"About the year 1713, not far from a tumulus at Elm, an urn full of small Roman brass coins, most of them of Victorinus and Petricus, was taken up ; and a Roman altar, 26 inches high and 14 broad (Cole's MSS.), is said to have been found at the same place. Also coins of Roman emperors from Gallienus down to Gratian were found in this parish, and deposited with Beauprè Bell, Esq., who has given an account thereof" (*Bib. Top.* iii. p. 169).

Concerning the further course of the road it may be well to quote the remarks of Stukeley as follows : " I suppose this road passed the Wisbech river above the town towards Guyhurn Chapel, [probably at or near to Cold Harbour,] then went to Trokenholt and Clow's Cross, ... from thence in a straight line to Spalding; by this means most of the square forts in [the Wapentake of] Elloe, where Roman antiquities were discovered, together with most of the southern hamlets, will be found to be situated near or upon it." Concerning the places thus noticed he states as follows: "At Gedney Hill several Roman coins have been found, some of Antoninus. In the same hamlet, about two miles north of Southsea bank, is a pasture called the High Doles, being a square doubly moated, where ancient foundations have been dug up and some Roman coins. Another like square so moated is in the parish of [Sutton] St Edmunds, about the same distance from the said bank where the like matters have been discovered. Aswich Grange [doubtless Aswichtoft] in Whaplode Drove parish [where Roman coins are still found (*Rep. &c. of Assoc. Archit. Soc.* i. 341)] is a high piece of ground square and moated about: in this and near it many Roman coins have been dug up, and urns, which I have seen. In the parish of Fleet near Ravensclough, about 1698, upon a piece of high ground where buildings had been, Mr Edw. Lenton dug up a large urn with letters round it, full of Roman coins, about the quantity of three pecks, ... they were of brass piled edgeways, mostly of the time of Gallienus and the thirty tyrants so called, Tetricus, Claudius Gothicus, Victorinus, Carausius, Allectus, &c." (Stuk. *Itin. Cur.* i. 11 and 13).

A road supposed to have crossed this at Elm and led to Wisbech, &c., will be described presently.

10. SUFFOLK AND SAWTRY WAY.—Several portions of this road are still in use, and are called the *Suffolk Way* to the south of the fens, and *Sawtry Way* to the north of them. It came from London to Dunmow (CÆSAROMAGUS?) by Wixoe, where it crossed the *Via Devana*, to Straddishall, by a very direct course, but perhaps threw off a loop route near Stambourne, by Ridgewell and Clare to Straddishall. It then seems

to have changed its direction from north-east to a little to the west of north; passing by Lidgate, where Roman bricks and a coin of Alexander Severus have been found, and at a little beyond which place it forms the boundary of the counties of Suffolk and Cambridge, and bears the name of *Suffolk Way;* near Ouseden, from whence coins of Lucilia and Salonina have been obtained by the Cambridge Antiquarian Society. Passing to the east of Newmarket it seems to have gone through Chippenham Park to Fordham, along Brook Street to Soham, where on a piece of ground resembling an island in the fen seven or eight urns were found (Sir W. Dugdale in a letter to Sir T. Brown, 1658, in Brown's *Posth. Works,* 4), and with a raised gravel crest, along Soham Causeway to Ely. This raised part or causeway is believed to have been made, I should rather say repaired, for the first Bishop of Ely by a monk named John. (Ledger Book of Ely as quoted by Dugdale, *Embank.* cap. 41). In those times it was not unfrequent to say that a road was made by some one, when in fact it was only restored from a state of extreme decay upon the former foundation. Mr Litchfield informs me that he has a Roman fibula and spear-head from Soham Fen.

I suspect that it left Ely along the high lands by Alderforth (perhaps Old Road) to Witchford, then passing a little to the north of Sutton (South Town) to Bury Steads, where it descended into the fen, and probably emerged again, after a distance of five miles, at Colne, the name of which shows that it probably is a Roman site.

Mr Hartshorne (*Salop. Antiq.* 273) proposes a different course for this, which he calls the *Sawtry Way.* He commences it at Thetford, 2½ miles south of Ely, and believes it to have passed by Stretham, Wilburton and Haddenham, where Roman vessels have been found (Cambridge Antiquarian Museum); Earith, where fragments of Roman pottery were found in a field on his land, and given to the Wisbech Museum by Mr John Brown, a respected member of the Society of Friends, in 1848. What seem to have been British remains, such as "a dagger," are also mentioned by him as having been obtained from near the river Ouse at Earith. He has in his possession a "Roman figure in brass, about 9 inches in height," found there, and states, in a letter with which he has favoured me, that querns have been met with: also in the same field where the pottery lay he found a "square of about 16 feet, set with common pebbles, about 2 feet below the soil, with a pebbled path leading from it;" also a coin of Commodus. Thence to Needingworth and the neighbourhood of St Ives, whence it was continued along what is still called the *Sawtry Way*, and which commences at about one mile to the west of St Ives. Should this be the correct view, it may have approached the river Ouse from Soham by crossing the narrow fen to Barraway, which is on high land and just opposite to Thetford. Even under this supposition it seems highly probable that the line from Ely to Colne is also ancient.

It is worthy of remark that there is another drier but circuitous route by which Thetford may be reached from Fordham, viz. by keeping along the top of the narrow ridge of so-called "highland" by Wicken and Spinny Abbey to Fordey, and thence crossing the river to Thetford. The word Fordey, or Road Island, as it probably may be translated, is suggestive. On my supposition that this road went to Colne, it must have divided into two branches; one going to the neighbourhood of St Ives[1] to be continued along the *Sawtry Way*, as would also be the case on Mr Hartshorne's plan, the other proceeding to Bury, near Ramsey. Doubtless there was some road from Bury to the *Erming Street* and *Via Devana*, and as much of the country lying to the west of Bury must have been very difficult to traverse, it seems not unlikely

[1] Gorham states (St Neots, 15), on the authority of Hutchinson's MS. on Huntingdonshire, that there was a Roman post at Holywell near St Ives. He says that there was a chain of forts on the Ouse, viz. Sandy, Eynesbury, Godmanchester, and Holywell. The first three are well known; the last I now hear of for the first time.

that a road was directed towards Huntingdon, and perhaps also went to a ford at or near Hemingford or Holywell, so as to communicate with the *Via Devana*, which passes at not more than a mile to the south of the river at the former place. If this ford was at Holywell, the way probably passed by Swavesey; but if, as seems far more probable, the Ouse was crossed at Hemingford, it is likely that the connecting track was continued beyond the way to Cambridge, along what is now called the *Moat's Way*, by Littlebury to Latenbury on the *Erming Street*, and possibly may have even extended by Graveley to join the road to Sandy.

The modern *Sawtry Way* is a straight line of road commencing on Houghton Hill, and passing by King's and Abbot's Ripton and Wood Walton to join the *Erming Street* or *Stangate*, near Sawtry.

Mr Litchfield has a small sacrificial cup made of bronze of about six inches in height, with two handles formed in imitation of the caduceus of Mercury, and on each side a centaur, one of which is playing upon a pipe. It was found in the deep cutting made for the railroad, near Somersham, a few years since.

At a later period there seems to have been considerable communication across the Ouse near St Ives, which caused the contiguous villages of Hemingford Grey and Abbots to spring up on the south side, and Wyton and Houghton similarly on the northern side of the river.

11. ALDRETH CAUSEWAY.—There is an ancient road which each of these routes crosses at right angles: in one instance near Witcham, and in the other at Haddenham. As much of this road as is nearly certainly ancient is almost parallel to the *Akeman Street*, and served, like it, as a way from the drier lands near Cambridge to the islands in the fen. Before the diversion of the waters of the Ouse from what is now called the Old Ouse or Old West River to the magnificent artificial cuts known as the Bedford Rivers, the access to those

islands must have been always difficult and often nearly impossible. The Romans reached them by means of the road from Cambridge to Ely, crossing the river and its accompanying fen near Stretham; and their judgment in selecting this route is shown by its having continued with little interruption, and with only slight deviations from its line, to be the principal way into the Isle of Ely up to the present time. At a late period of the middle ages, and until the modern causeway near Stretham was formed, a track starting from Cottenham and crossing the West River at Twenty-pence Ferry communicated with Wilburton. Proceeding up the old valley of the Ouse we next arrive at the road first mentioned in this paragraph. It is probably first seen at about halfway between Rampton and Willingham, at a spot marked by a sort of square on the Ordnance Map [1]. From that place it may be faintly traced to Balsar's Hill; a large circular camp, the ramparts of which have been much lowered since the enclosure of the district, and seem to be gradually disappearing under the plough. This camp is supposed to derive its name from Belasis, a commander under King William I., and may have been occupied by him during the war between that king and the Saxons collected in the Isle of Ely. It seems improbable that he made it; and if *Aldreth Causeway* is Roman, as some believe, then Balsar's Hill was probably a British fort occupied by the Roman troops. From Balsar's Hill to Aldreth the road is more distinct. It crosses the Old Ouse at High Bridge, and from thence to Aldreth is called *Aldreth Causeway* [2]. This causeway, although now but little used, was once of such consequence that (as I learn from my friend the Rev. S. Banks, Rector of Cottenham, but formerly resident at Haddenham)

---

[1] This spot is now altered by enclosure, and there is nothing left to account for its singular form at the time when the map was made.

[2] It is scarcely necessary to remind antiquaries that Aldreth is a corruption of Etheldreda, the foundress of the abbey of Ely. This name adds, in my opinion, to the probability that William I. found a road here, and did not make it, as some have supposed.

various parishes in the fens are liable to provide for the repair of small parts of it respectively. From Aldreth the road is continued by what is called the *Sand Way* to Haddenham, and probably extended to Witcham, or even further. It is not improbable that this line of communication was connected at its southern end with Cambridge, along what is now called Cuckoo Lane, and by the village of Histon. Country people inform me that, before the inclosure, there was an old road that diverged to the right from the *Via Devana* at How House, and led to Histon: this may have been the original line to Cambridge.

At Rampton, about $1\frac{1}{2}$ mile to the south of Balsar's Hill, there is a curious quadrangular mound defended by a deep and broad ditch, and also an outer bank upon three of its sides. It is called Giant's Hill, and its use is not apparent.

A small Roman urn was found at Rampton in 1843 (Camb. Antiq. Museum). At Cottenham, which lies at about halfway between this road and the *Akeman Street*, a fourth brass coin of Gratianus, a small Roman urn, the neck of a large vase, and part of an amphora have been found (Camb. Antiq. Museum). At Over, distant about two miles from the other side of this road, a denarius of Faustina the elder has been found; and recently a great number of the copper coins of the lower empire, were obtained by Mr J. Symons, in the remains of a metal box. As far as could be made out they appeared to be mostly coins of Constantine, as I am informed by Mr E. Litchfield. Also chains of complicated construction and apparently Roman, one having large hooks attached, probably for hanging meat, the other intended to suspend a camp-kettle, were found at a depth of about five feet in Over fen, in 1850 (Camb. Antiq. Museum). At Coveney, which is not far from Witcham, the beautiful British shields described in the ' Publications' of the Society, and preserved in its Museum, were found.

Bury.—As it is believed that the station at Bury has not

been described, it is desirable to introduce some account of it here. The village of Bury is situated at about a mile to the south of Ramsey in Huntingdonshire. The station is a little to the south of the church on a slight elevation called May Hill, but is not now to be easily traced. The eastern side nearly corresponds with the hedge by the road to Warboys, and is raised several feet above the road by scarping the slope of the hill. The northern end of this bank is occupied by the hedge, but in its southern half the hedge is placed at its base. The southern side of the station is to the north of a hedge at its eastern, and to the south of it at its western end. The western side is divided into two parts by the shape of the hill and the boggy ground at its base. It is formed with a terrace placed against the base, or rather cut out, of the hill just above the marsh, through which a brook flows at a short distance. The parts of this side are nearly straight, and are connected by a curve; along the whole of it the terrace is to be traced. The northern side appears now to be occupied by a hedge, but cannot be clearly made out. The inclosed space is large, being fully a furlong in length from north to south, but less from east to west, and narrower in its northern than its southern half. It is commandingly situated, and must have had great strength. Its interior rises into a considerable hill for this flat district, and its highest point is capped by a large tumulus with a cup-shaped top. With the slight exception of the parts on the outside of the eastern and southern hedges, the whole forms one grass field, and does not appear to have ever been under the plough. See plan Plate 4.

12. BURY TO WISBECH AND SPALDING.—There is reason to suspect that a Roman road went from Bury, perhaps along an embankment crossing Bury Plashes to Ramsey; then by Cold Harbour, near Ramsey Mere to Benwick, where Roman coins have been found (Stukeley, *Car.* ii. 139); then by Appleborough, near Doddington, where, in 1821, some copper coins of the Emperors Decentius and Constantius were

found (Watson's *Wisbech*, 585); there has also been a recent discovery of a large quantity of Roman pottery at Wimblington, on the line of the railway, and near to it, as Mr W. E. Rose informs me; he also tells me that near the same spot a vase was turned up by the plough in 1848, containing at least 2000 copper coins in a very decomposed state. Mr Rose states that, "curiously enough the bottom of the vase contained a piece of lead evidently run into it in a liquid state, the size and thickness being equal to a twopenny piece." He adds that "the whole of this locality [near Doddington] has produced Roman and British antiquities." The track went by March, where, near to the church, there is a square entrenchment, having Burrow Moor and Burrow Farm adjoining it. It next crossed the *Fen Road*, and passing Coldham, where Mr Rose states, in the letter with which he has favoured me, that drain-pipes and other Roman fragments have been found; and Waldersey, where a Roman vase was found in 1845. Also at the latter place, in the year 1785, "an earthen pot containing a considerable quantity of small copper coins, chiefly of Valentinian and Arcadius, was dug up (Watson's *Wisbech*, 507, and 508); and in 1845 a large Roman vase was found in Waldersey Fen, and presented to the Wisbech Museum by Mr W. Jecks, where most of the above-mentioned antiquities are also preserved.

At and near to Wisbech many Roman coins have occurred. An aureus of Valentinian, found in 1845, is in the Cambridge Antiquarian Museum. In the Wisbech Museum there are Roman coins found on the North Brink, and a Roman vase found in a field at South Brink, and coins from other parts of the neighbourhood. Beyond Wisbech the road passed on at a short distance within the Roman sea-bank by Newton, where coins of Gallienus occurred in about the year 1787 (Watson's *Wisbech*, 487), and more recently of Victorinus; by Tydd St Mary, near to which place at Tydd Gout a vase was found in the Roman sea-bank, and is now in the Wisbech Museum,

Long Sutton and Fleet, to Spalding. My information concerning this part of the road is derived from a paper in the
Reports, &c. of the Associated Architectural Societies (i. 340),
in which it is described, and stated to be "probably the old
British path on the borders of the marsh, it being still at Fleet
called Haregate or Hergate. In the old terriars the road
has the same name to Spalding. A part of this road at and
beyond Moulton was originally a little to the north of the
present road, and is still called Old Spalding Gate;" otherwise
it corresponds with the modern road.

It must be confessed that the whole of the above line of
supposed road is chiefly founded upon probability and the discovery of antiquities. The undoubted existence of Roman sea-
banks on the coast of the Wash, show that this district was
considered of value at that period. Dugdale was fully convinced that the sea board of Marshland and Holland was
gained from the sea by the Romans (*Embanking*, cap. 34).
At Walsoken near Wisbech, and close to the Roman sea-
bank, two coins of Constantine were found, and presented to
the Wisbech Museum (*Camb. Chron.*, March 2, 1850). At
Walpole St Peter, a few miles to the north of Wisbech, and
also close to these sea-banks, Mr E. Cony stated that a tenant
of his, "who lives under the bank, upon digging in his garden,
about three feet under ground, found many Roman bricks,
and an aqueduct made with earthen pipes. These pipes were
made of pale reddish earth, and grew hard again upon their
being exposed some time to the air; the length of these was
20 inches, the bow $3\frac{3}{4}$ inches, the thickness of their sides half
an inch, one of the ends much smaller than the other." (*In
a letter from E. Cony, Esq., to R. Gale, Esq., dated Nov.* 8,
1727, *in Bibl. Topog. Brit. (Reliq. Gal.)* iii. 49).

A spear, the umbo of a shield, an earthen vessel, and a
glass drinking-cup, similar to those figured by Mr C. R. Smith,
(*Collectanea Antiqua*, ii. t. 51), were found at Chatteris, on a
slightly elevated spot near Somersham [now called Chatteris]

Ferry. They are described and figured in the *Gentleman's Magazine* (xxxvi. 119), by Dr Stukeley, and although called British by him were undoubtedly Saxon remains. " In 1824, an earthen vessel, which contained about 1000 small copper coins, chiefly of Constantius, many of Constans and Constantine, and a few with the ... emblem of Romulus and Remus suckled by the wolf, was ploughed up near the [same] ferry, two miles from the town, on the site of the ancient river or West Water" (Watson's *Wisbech*, 578).

A large Roman vase was found at Chatteris in 1830, and a small sepulchral vase containing ashes in 1819, both of which were presented to the Wisbech Museum by Mr J. Girdlestone; also in the course of the works for the railroad near to that place, a large vase containing bones was dug up and given to that museum by Mr W. E. Rose.

Near the road leading from Somersham to Chatteris, an urn with Roman coins, and others with 60 coins of the later emperors, were found in 1731 (Gough's *Camden*, 159). And Dr Stukeley states (*Reliq. Gal. in Bibl. Topog. Brit.* iii. 115) that Roman coins and antiquities have been found at Somersham.

At Cold Harbour, which is close to what was Ramsey Mere, this supposed road appears to have divided, a branch towards the north being called *Cnut's Dyke*, which will be noticed presently.

13. THE BULLOCK ROAD.—For convenience I have employed this name to denote a road extending from Verulamium to Chesterton on the Nen, with a branch to Godmanchester; although it only bears that denomination in a part of its course, which may perhaps rightly be considered as a British Way rather than a Roman Street. It is hoped that this extension of the name will not be considered as very objectionable, when it is remembered that there is no name for the part of it which was certainly used, and perhaps much improved, by the Romans. It scarcely touches our county,

but as some miles of it appear on the map it ought to be noticed here. If we commence at Baldock, where it crossed the *Icknield Way*, we find it to have nearly coincided with the modern turnpike-road for many miles to Biggleswade. At less than a mile from Baldock we arrive at Norton Bury, where, as has been already stated, a road to Shefford probably branched from it. A few miles in advance there is a Caldecote near to it on the right; and at a few miles further we meet with Stratton. Due east of Biggleswade it crosses the *Akeman Street*, and leaving Road Farm a little to the right the modern road deserts it, and it follows the line of a fence, but is nearly or quite effaced for about a mile. It then reappears by a tumulus near to Fursdon Hall, and may be seen crossing the marshy land to Stratford and Chesterfield (or Chesterton, as named hy Gorham), the site of SALENÆ. On the opposite side of the river Ivel there are again two Caldecotes. On Galley Hill, above Stratford, there is a small square Roman fort (probably that called Chesterton by Stukeley, *Itin. Cur.* 74), very strongly situated, as the sandy hill slopes abruptly from its ramparts on three of the sides. Separated from this fort by a narrow and deep valley is a point of elevated land, which is nearly surrounded by abrupt slopes, and has a very deep trench and lofty embankment drawn across the narrow neck, which connects it with the adjoining elevated district. Exactly opposite to the camp on Galley Hill there is a ford of the river Ivel, which was defended on its western side by the ancient ramparts called Beeston Berrys, of which there are now only faint traces to be seen. It is uncertain what was the exact site of SALENÆ; and indeed as the space between the hills and the marshes is narrow, it may have been of considerable length, and trusted for its defence to the fortifications on the higher ground above it. My friend Mr Arthur Taylor places it at the spot occupied by the railway station, above which there is an irregular hill-top fortified along its curved edge by a tolerably strong rampart, but quite open at

its eastern side, where it adjoins the hill-country. This place is
called Cæsar's Camp, but was probably a temporary British
post. If the station was at the place supposed by Mr Taylor,
the road probably ascended the hill through a hollow on its
north-western side. The Roman station is more usually placed
at Chesterfield, about a quarter of a mile to the south of the
railway station; and Dr Bennet states (Lysons' *Bedford*, 27)
that " from the north-east side of the station, near the banks
of the Ivel, this road continues through a small valley, leaving
the British camp above-mentioned [Cæsar's Camp] on the
left-hand, and another hill which has been dug up for a stone-
quarry on the right, straight to a hedge-row, which runs
down through a piece of land to a small copse in the bottom
[probably Hawksbury Wood], thence it continues equally
straight, first as a boundary between Mr Pym's land and
Sandy field [the Hasell Hedge], and then entering some enclosures crosses the road to Everton and Tempsford, then
passes through a farm-yard, leaving the house [Gibraltar] to
the left, and through some more enclosures to a farm-house
[Low Farm, which is in Cambridgeshire,] which stands upon
it, then through another enclosure to Tempsford Marsh [where
there is a Cold Harbour a little on the right] ; after passing
which it ascends the hill close to a barrow or tumulus, almost
the invariable attendant on Roman roads." This tumulus is
now destroyed, and its exact site unknown. Taking up the
account of the road from this place, as given by Gorham
(*St Neots*, pp. 3 and 4), and starting from Crane Hill, upon
some part of which this tumulus stood, it bears north-east,
" leaving the manor farm of Puttock's Hardwich and Lans-
bury grounds a little on the west, it forms the boundary between Eynesbury and Abbotsley parishes. ... It crosses the
road from St Neots to Cambridge close to the village of
Weal; the main road being cut off from its course, and forming an elbow of about 200 yards upon the very line of the
Roman Street." Soon afterwards it forms the boundary of

Cambridge and Huntingdon shires near Graveley, and then
bears directly for Godmanchester. Mr Gorham justly remarks,
that "it is not to be distinguished by an elevated crest...the
repeated action of the plough has completely obliterated its
former character; it consequently presents to the eye nothing
more than an ordinary field-track." It does not seem to have
entered the hexagonal station at Godmanchester, but passing
along its western side, as the *Via Devana* did along the
north-eastern, combined with it and the *Erming Street* to
cross the Ouse. This is the Roman line, and we have now
to endeavour to trace the British Way, which probably separated from it at a little to the south of Puttock's Hardwich, if
indeed it did not continue along the valley from Sandy, and
went to Eynesbury, then crossed the Ouse probably at Eaton
ford and went by Stirtlow (Streetlow?), Buckden, Brampton
Hut, where it was crossed by the *Via Devana*, to Alconbury
Weston[1]. For about a mile beyond that place, the exact
line that it followed is not known. It then commences being
called by the name of the *Bullock Road* at Upton, and soon
passes by Coppingford and Cold Harbour. After advancing
five miles we find another Cold Harbour, immediately after
passing which the road crosses to the west of Billing Brook,
thereby departing from the right course to Chesterton. Probably it originally kept to the eastern side of the brook, and
arrived at Chesterton by the "convenient ridge of high ground"
mentioned by Horsley (*Brit. Rom.* 431). It is also probable
that this part of the ancient road obtained its present name
from being used by the drovers taking their cattle along it on
the way to the great market at St Ives. It is well known
that they always followed the grassy parish-roads, when in
their power, so as to avoid toll-gates and obtain ways more
suited to the feet of cattle than the hard turnpike-roads.

[1] Near Hail Weston, on the way to Great Stoughton and to the
south of the road, a bronze figure of Mercury is recorded by the Rev.
G. C. Gorham to have been found. He gives a map of the remains
in that neighbourhood. (*Archæol.* xxi. 550, t. 27.)

14. CNUT'S DYKE.—This now forms the foundation of the road from Bodsey near Ramsey to Pond's Bridge, and was continued by Horsey Hill and Standground to Peterborough. It runs by the side of Cnut's, or Suard's, or Oakley's, Delph, and also bears those names. It forms the boundary of Cambridgeshire throughout nearly the whole of its course. Reynolds (*Anton.* 258) says that it was a paved causeway. It is older than the time of Cnut (as is shown below under the head of Car Dyke), and is very probably Roman.

IV. ANCIENT DITCHES.

The four remarkable ancient ditches which are found in the southern part of Cambridgeshire are well deserving of attention, both from the grandeur of execution which is seen in two of them—for they are, it is believed, the strongest boundary ditches to be found in the kingdom—and from the remarkably skilful manner in which they have been planned so as to serve the purpose of their makers, and at the same time be of the least extent possible. From the fact that the elevated rampart is certainly on the western side of three of them, it may be stated with confidence that they were made by the inhabitants of the district now forming the counties of Norfolk and Suffolk, as a defence against the attacks of the people of the interior. If it is really the fact that the Roman roads have been cut through the ditches in at least three places, as is stated to be the case by several of the older antiquaries who saw them at a time when inclosure had not altered the surface of the country as is now the case, nor the turnpike-roads been formed which represent the ancient Roman or British lines of way, and when therefore there was far more certainty to be attained concerning the line of these ways; if, I repeat, the Romans did cut through the banks and fill up the ditches to make their roads, then of course the ditches were formed anteriorly to the complete Roman settlement of this district.

Some persons have supposed that they were made by the fol-
lowers of Boadicea, others that they were the work of invaders,
perhaps Belgæ, to secure the district conquered from the former
Celtic inhabitants. It seems nearly if not quite impossible
to lay down the course of the *Icknield Way*, and the Roman
Road which undoubtedly succeeded it, so as to avoid crossing
one or more of these ditches; and had the ditches been works
of a later time than the roads, we could hardly expect to have
found the gaps cut exactly upon the line of the roads, as seems
to be the case with that near Pampisford, even if so much
cannot be said with certainty concerning those in the Balsham
and Devil's ditches.

However that may be, there is no doubt that in the Saxon
period they formed the boundary between East Anglia and
Mercia, and that the easternmost of them marked the limit of
the halidome of St Edmund's Abbey at Bury, in the time of
King Cnut. Until recently also it was the boundary of the
diocess of Norwich. Each of these ditches extending from
fen or marshy land to a wooded country, and quite crossing
the narrow open district which formed the march of these ter-
ritories, and by which alone East Anglia could be approached
without great difficulty, must have presented a formidable ob-
stacle to the usual predatory inroads which constituted so large
a part of the warfare of those ages.

1. THE DEVIL'S DITCH.—This is the most easterly of
these remarkable works, and by far the greatest although not
the longest of them. It extends across Newmarket Heath
from the fens at Reche to the woodlands at Camois Hall near
Wood Ditton (Ditch town), and is nearly straight throughout,
lying from north-west to south-east. It is very perfect, but
more especially so at the end nearest to Reche and in the
neighbourhood of Stetchworth Park. Many gaps have been
cut through it by filling up the ditch with the materials of the
bank, and it is now impossible to determine at what dates they
were made. One called the Running Gap probably allowed

the ancient road (named above the *Peddar Way*) from Chesterford to Exning to pass; but concerning this I must refer to the remarks already made. Another permitted the *Icknield Way* to pass; and the others have been made for purposes which it is not now easy to point out. The first mention of it with which I am acquainted is that King Edward fought a battle near to it (inter duo fossata sancti Eadmundi) in the year 902, as recorded by Matthew of Westminster (*Flores Hist.* fol. 268). The other ditch was doubtless the Balsham Dyke. According to measurements made by Sir H. Dryden and communicated to the Rev. C. H. Hartshorne, the bank is 18 feet above the level of the country, 30 feet above the bottom of the ditch, and 12 feet in width at the top; the width of the ditch is 20 feet; the length of the slope of the bank on its eastern side is 30 feet, and that of the bank and ditch together 46 feet[1]. In its more perfect parts it probably is very nearly of its original form and size, as its surface has apparently never been disturbed since the turf first grew over it. At Stetchworth there is a rather large and almost square camp close to its western side, which may have been Roman. At Reche coins of Constans, and of the type bearing URBS ROMA, have been found; in Bottisham Fen, Roman vessels and also bronze fibulæ; in Burwell Fen, Roman vessels and a coin of Alexander Severus. These places lie north and south, and at a short distance from Reche.

2. THE FLEAM OR BALSHAM DYKE.—This is seven miles to the west of the Devil's Ditch. It is not straight like

---

[1] These measurements differ considerably from those made by Mr A. J. Kempe, F.S.A., and communicated to the Society of Antiquaries in March, 1843. He states that at a little to the south of the Cambridge and Newmarket Road "the vallum presents an escarpment inclined at an angle of 70 degrees, which, measured along the slope, is 90 feet in length. On the top of the vallum is a cursus or way about 18 feet in width." (*Camb. Chron.* 22 Apr. 1843). The ditch is certainly very different in its proportions in different parts, and may have been so originally. I am inclined to prefer Sir H. Dryden's measurements as being nearest to the truth.

the Devil's Ditch, but considerably curved in several parts of its course, to meet the requirements of the ground. It commenced at Fen Ditton (named, as was Wood Ditton, from the ditch), probably close to the river Cam, just below the church, and may still be traced along the road to Quy, which is formed in part below its bank and in part upon it. At Quy bridge we lose sight of it, indeed Wilbraham Fen was a sufficient defence from that point until we arrive at Great Wilbraham. At about half a mile to the south of the latter place it commences again, and may be followed (although much reduced by cultivation) running due south to Shardlow's Well, near Fulbourn. It then shows itself in all its greatness, and continues in beautiful preservation for several miles to the south-east, until approaching Balsham it is again much injured The depth of this ditch from the top of the bank is now, in its best preserved part, about 20 feet. The detached part near Ditton is not quite two miles in length, but the other portion, extending from Wilbraham to Balsham, is not less than six miles long. It crosses the supposed line of the *Icknield Way* near to a tumulus called Mutlow Hill, and is said to have been filled up to allow it to pass; but of that, however probable it may be, there is no proof. As has been already stated, the *Peddar Way* seems to have passed it at the point where it forms an angle at Shardlow's Well, and where also it has been levelled at some former period.

Here again we have a line of defence drawn from the woodlands across an open chalky district to the fens. We also see how advantage was taken of the fenny spot near Wilbraham to avoid the necessity of making about two miles of artificial defence. It must be remembered that at the ancient period when these ditches were made, the fens consisted probably of a series of islands surrounded by morasses and lakes, although not so wet as they became in the middle ages from the silting up of the outfalls of the rivers which pass through them; that a nearly detached piece of fen, like that at Wil-

braham, was almost always flooded; and that the Cam and
other rivers ran for many miles above the true fen districts
through a continuous, although often narrow, line of marshes[1].
If then a fortification was made extending from the edge of
the fen, or of the fenny banks of the Cam, or one of its tribu-
taries, across the open belt of country until it reached the
extensive woodlands lying towards the south-east, a very perfect
security would be obtained against the cattle-driving propensi-
ties of the neighbours of those who made the ditch. We have
seen that this is what was done in the case of the two ditches
already noticed, and such will also be found to be the fact in
the two instances which remain to be described.

3. THE BRENT OR PAMPISFORD DITCH.—This is only
about one mile and three quarters in length, and of slight
depth. It begins at a place called Brent-ditch End at Pampisford, and extends in a nearly south-east direction through
the plantations of Pampisford Hall. It may be traced to a
spot close to Abington Park, but did not quite certainly ter-
minate there, for considerable changes have been made in the
arrangement of the ground: as, however, the woodland commenced thereabouts it probably did not extend much beyond
that spot. Mr Hartshorne says that "it has no bank on either
side," but that "the vallum was on the same side as that of
the other dykes," viz. the eastern. I do not quite understand
this remark, but a recent examination of it near Pampisford
Hall, where it is in the best preservation, has shown that there
is still a low but well-marked bank on its *western* side, and no
trace of one on the eastern. In the winter when the trees are
leafless this is well seen. The turnpike-road which now represents the *Icknield Way* crosses it, and the ditch is filled
up by the side of the road. This might be taken for the place

[1] A good idea of the fen islands may be obtained from the map,
derived from a survey made in the year 1604, and published in
Colonel John Armstrong's *History of the Navigation of the Port of
King's Lynn and of Cambridge.* Fol. London, 1767.

where the old way crossed, was it not known (as I learn from W. P. Hamond, Esq. of Pampisford Hall) to be of recent formation. Dr Mason states (Gough's *Camden*, 141), that "towards the middle it has been filled up for the *Icknield Way* to pass over it ;" and the spot referred to by him must be the site of the present road, as there is no other gap.

At Brent-ditch End a marshy district commences, which is connected with and continued along the course of the river Grant, or Cam, until it joins the great level of the fens.

4. THE BRAN OR HAYDON DITCH.—It commences at the southern end of a tract of fen called Melbourn Common (which is connected with a branch of the river Cam) just at the spot where the brook that flows through the common rises at several beautiful springs. At that point its rampart and fosse are still very conspicuous, but the latter is rendered less apparent by a hedge having been planted in it. Although in many parts much obliterated by cultivation, it may be traced over the slightly undulating country for about two miles to Haydon Grange, and then up the hill for another mile to the village of Haydon. The probable continuation of the *Ashwell Street* crossed it at a very short distance from the fen, but is now obliterated by the enclosure and cultivation of the district. At about a mile in advance it is crossed by the turnpike-road between Foulmire and Barley, which is the road mentioned above as supposed to be of Roman origin by Stukeley. Close to this road the rampart still retains its coating of turf. Soon afterwards it crosses another road, which is probably ancient, and may have been a second track of the *Icknield Way*, which it leaves at about three miles to the east of Royston, and again rejoins at Worsted Lodge. It then immediately enters Essex, and soon after passing Haydon Grange crosses the *Icknield Way* and ascends the hill to Haydon, at which place the ancient woodlands commenced. The measurements of this ditch are very difficult to determine, owing to the destructive agency of time, and more especially of agriculture. In places

the rampart has at least 7 feet of vertical elevation above the fosse. The rampart is on the eastern side. On the whole this ditch is, like the three already described, a very remarkable and interesting work.

Mr R. C. Neville discovered on the summit of the hill at Haydon a chamber. "At the depth of 4 feet [the workmen] struck on three walls built with bricks of solid clunch chalk, so as to present a longitudinal *cul de sac*. On clearing this of loose soil (apparently some kind of ash) the chamber appeared about 10 feet deep from the top, 9 long by 5 broad; the centre being occupied by a species of altar in solid clunch, attached to the end wall at the narrow or cross wall. All round three sides of this there was a passage with just room to squeeze round between it and the wall on the three sides; in the centre of this, on the floor, there was a gutter 3 inches in diameter. The remains taken from this excavation were: a good bronze bracelet, in good preservation; two or three iron instruments; one coin of Constantinus II., in brass; and a great many bullocks' horns" (*Jour. Archæol. Assoc.* iii. 340).

[5. DEVIL'S DYKE IN NORFOLK.—At the edge of my map there will be seen two detached ditches, or perhaps banks, for I have not seen them, called *Devil's Dyke*. Mr Woodward, in his map of Roman Norfolk, marks this as being a British road from Brandon by Oxburg to Narburgh Camp; but his view does not appear to be borne out by the course it seems really to take. It has more probably been a line of defence, like the Cambridgeshire ditches; for it commences abruptly at the river side at Brandon, not being discoverable on the south side of the fen, and towards the north it terminates at the fenny district of the Stoke River, near Cranwick: this is the southern part called *Foss* or *Devil's Dyke*. The northern part, also called *Devil's Dyke*, appears similarly to cross a dry district between fens. It probably commenced at Beachamwell by the fen side, not at Oxburg, which lies to the south of this fen district, and extended to Narburgh on the fen by the side of the river Nar. See Map in the *Archæologia*, xxiii., or Woodward's *Norwich Castle*.]

V. THE CAR DYKE.

To the north of Peterborough the ancient ditch or canal called the *Car Dyke* is well known, and therefore, as that district is altogether out of our county, no description of that part of it is requisite in this treatise. Its channel is stated to have there been 60 feet in width, with a broad flat bank upon each side (*Rep. &c. of Assoc. Archit. Soc.* i. 338).

To the south of Peterborough the state of things is very different: indeed it may be doubted if any antiquary, except Stukeley, has felt convinced that it really did extend into Cambridgeshire.

The origin of the *Car Dyke* is altogether unknown, although it is perhaps rightly ascribed to the Romans. Stukeley thought that " Car" was a contraction of Carausius, to whom he referred nearly every ancient work in this part of England. If we could see any proof that he did perform even a small part of what Stukeley attributes to him, he would indeed deserve to be considered as a benefactor of the country, and lauded as was done by his above-named historian. We appear to know very little concerning him ; the history of his time being lost : and it seems peculiarly bold to attempt the compilation of an account of his reign from his coins alone. It cannot be denied that Stukeley has shewn singular ingenuity in the attempt that he made to do this, and the extensive learning and large collection of facts recorded in his book must always make it of great value to the antiquary.

Stukeley, as has been already stated, called Cambridge GRANTA, and supposed that it was founded by Carausius at the southern end of the *Car Dyke*, which he considered either to have been made, or, at any rate, restored by him from a useless state. He supposed it to have been formed to act as a navigable canal from the corn-country[1] of this part of England to York. He states that the same Emperor established Stourbridge Fair as part of this great plan of internal communication[2]. I confess that this, and many other things in the *Medallic History of Carausius*, are quite beyond my powers of belief.

But to proceed to the consideration of the supposed southern part of the *Car Dyke*. It seems highly probable that there was a navigable cut through the district forming the edge of the fens, and one of the courses laid down by Stukeley may very likely belong to it. Of the two routes to be found described in his works, it is best totally to neglect that given in Part I. (pp. 199, 200) of the *Medallic History*, for in Part II. (p. 137), which was published several years after the first part of that work, he has quite changed his views on the subject, and reverted nearly to the account which he had long before given in his *Paleographia*. He says, "just below Cambridge the artificial cut opens into the river, runs along the side of it, taking the benefit of higher water, for half a mile" (*Car.* 199); and it may be presumed, therefore, that he supposed it to commence near Milton. "A little above Waterbeach," as he

---

[1] The emperor Julian, according to his own written testimony, (*Orat. ad S. P. Q. Atheniensem*) employed no less than six hundred vessels in the exportation of corn and flour to supply the towns and fortresses on the Rhine at about the middle of the fourth century. To meet a sudden call of this kind the cultivation of Britain must have been far more general in the time of the Romans than we moderns have usually been inclined to allow. Gibbon (ed. 1825. ii. 427) thought that each vessel might be of 70 tons' burthen (a very small allowance), and thus calculated that they were capable of exporting 120,000 quarters of grain.

[2] One of his remarks concerning this fair may amuse the readers of this treatise. He says, "Memorials of the antiquity of the fair, and of the religious observances there performed in Roman times, are kept up in several particulars; as of the Arch-flamen of Granta, in the Vice-Chancellor of the University, proclaiming it with much solemnity: of divine service, and a sermon celebrated in a pulpit set up for the purpose, on the two Sundays, in the chief part of the fair called the Duddery." (*Caraus.* i. 206.)

says in another place (*Paleog.* ii. 38), "begins our famous *Car Dyke*. The bed of this artificial cut is very plain from hence, quite across the fen, through Cottenham parish until it enters the Old Ouse." Along this river it passed to Earith. He then continues it "by Ramsey to Suard's Dyke; .... then the boats passed by Benwick, where Roman coins have been found; so by Whittlesey Mere, or some cut by the side of it, to Horsey Bridge, where Roman coins too are found, and so to Peterborough river" (*Paleog.* ii. 38). By this he probably means, that from Earith it followed the West Water to Benwick, near Ramsey Mere, but in Cambridgeshire. In the second part of the *Medallic History*, he says, that "at Waterbeach .....it begins with a fair and large artificial channel, proceeding by the windmill north-westward. The ditch now has water in it in several places. The inhabitants hereabouts have a notion that the Ouse from Audrey causeway passed anciently this way into Cambridge river..... It has not the least appearance of a natural river" (p. 133). Dugdale considered this as a branch of the Cam; his words are:—"The river Grant, by a fair channel passing from Beach to Chare Fen, in Cottenham, and so into Ouse, was diverted; and by a straighter course turned down by another branch of the same river to Harrimere, where it loseth the name" (*Embank.* 373). To return to Stukeley, "It runs by Chare fen in the parish of Cottenham.....and passes into the present river called the Old Ouse, going to the great wooden bridge upon Audrey causeway, whence it goes along the present channel of the river westwards to Earith" (*Car.* i. 133). "At Earith the *Car Dyke*, entering Huntingdonshire, crosses the Huntingdon river....., and proceeds northwards in that stream now called the West Water to Benwick, then by that stream called the Old Nen or Whittlesey Dyke" to Peterborough (*Car.* ii. 136). Notice has already been taken of *Cnut's Dyke*, which Stukeley supposed to have been a road in connexion with the navigation in this part of its course, and the *King Street* to have been of

5—2

similar use to the north of Peterborough. Dugdale remarks concerning the channel by the side of this road, that "about two miles distant from the north-east side of the above-specified mere [Whittlesey], there is a memorable channel cut through the body of the fen, extending itself from near Ramsey to Peterborough, and is called King's Delph. The common tradition is, that King Canutus, or his queen, being in some peril, in their passage from Ramsey to Peterborough, by reason of the boisterousness of the waves on Whittlesey Mere, caused this ditch to be first made. And therewith do some of our historians agree who say thus: 'Anno Domini mxxxiv. Cnuto, rex potentissimus, viam in marisco, inter Ramsey et Burgum, quod "King's Delph" dicitur, ut periculum magnorum stagnorum vitaretur, eruderavit' (Matth. Westm. *Annales*). But how to reconcile this testimony with what I meet with threescore years before, I know not; which is that King Edgar confirming to the monks of Peterborough the fourth part of Whittlesey Mere..... says [the boundaries extend] 'orientaliter ad King's Delph.'" (*Embank.* 363). After these long and rather complicated extracts, I must now leave my readers to form their own opinion concerning the probability of these very ancient cuts being part of a great plan of the Romans in continuation southward of the *Car Dyke*. It seems improbable that the Saxons can have made them at so early a period as that at which one part of them at least is shown to have existed; and the traditional name of King's Delph, in conjunction with the *King's Street* to the north, may add weight to the supposition of both being of Roman origin.

VI. OLD COURSE OF THE RIVERS.

BEFORE concluding this imperfect sketch of the ancient lines
of communication and earth-works of Cambridgeshire, it may
be desirable to point out the ancient course of the rivers that
pass through the fens. They are the Nen, the Great Ouse,
the Cam, and the Little Ouse rivers. The Nen on arriving at
Peterborough turned to the right, and making a circuit through
Whittlesey, Ugg and Ramsey Meres, passed then in a pretty
direct course by March to Wisbech. At Peterborough it
seems to have thrown off a branch to join the Welland near
Croyland.

The great Ouse enters the fens near Earith, at which place
it formerly forked, its chief branch flowing by Harrimere, Ely
and Littleport, then by what is now called the Welney river
to Wisbech, where, in conjunction with the Nen, its waters
reached the sea. The other branch of the Ouse is now called
the West Water, and ran from Earith to Benwick, where it
joined the main channel of the Nen. Both these channels are
now nearly or quite closed to the waters of the Ouse, which
are carried by the Bedford rivers in a direct line to Denver,
and there poured into the channel of the Little Ouse to reach
the sea at Lynn.

The Cam, although it changes its name to Ouse at Harrimere, where it originally joined that river on its way to
Wisbech, does now really extend by way of Ely and Prickwillow
to Denver; for, except in case of very great floods, not a drop
of Ouse water enters it before that place is reached.

The Little Ouse is the present channel of the Great Ouse
from Denver to Lynn.

It is thus seen that nearly all the water which reached the
great level found its natural outlet at Wisbech (a word reasonably derived from Ouse beach), where originally the channel

was deep enough to afford a natural drainage to the country. In process of time this outlet became choked, and the rivers changed their course or were diverted by artificial means.

I have now only to add an expression of my hope that this attempt may lead others far better qualified for the task than I can pretend to be, to follow up the study of the traces of the ancient inhabitants of our district, and to cause the production by some other member of the University of a more complete treatise on this interesting subject.

APPENDIX.

1. ROMAN INSCRIPTIONS.—Since the copies of Inscriptions given on pages 23 and 24 were printed, I have fortunately succeeded in finding the originals of them. The stones upon which they are inscribed have been placed under the left-hand archway leading to the University Schools. Their history was forgotten, and had there not been an account of them published in the *Gentleman's Magazine*, the chief interest attaching to the Inscriptions would have been destroyed. This interest is chiefly founded upon the fact, that they are believed to be the only Roman Inscriptions that have been discovered near to Cambridge.

This is an instructive example of the necessity that exists for the addition of some permanent record to antiquities, and other objects of interest deposited with public bodies.

The stones are not cylindrical, as is stated to be the case at page 23, and in the *Gentleman's Magazine,* but flattened with the angles rounded. The following are the measurements:

	No. 1.			No. 2.	
	ft.	in.		ft.	in.
Height	2	6	Height	2	8
Girth	3	4½	Girth	3	3
Width	1	0	Width	1	3
Thickness	0	8½	Thickness	0	6

It will be seen from these measurements that the stones are of very different shapes, and cannot have had any connexion with each other. They are therefore fragments of two distinct monuments which stood contiguously by the side of the so called *Via Devana.* They were found by Mr Henry L. Biden, at that time a student of Trinity Hall, projecting from a bank near the present high road, at a distance of nearly three miles from Cambridge, in the month of October 1812.

The Inscriptions are very easily read, although the stone is much decayed. In the case of No. 1 the lines all commence near the angle of the stone, upon one of its broader sides, and the first letters of each range vertically. The first and third lines extend beyond the front face of the block, and are continued round the angle on to the lateral face. The Inscription appears to be perfect, and was erected in honour of Constantinus Pius by the fifth legion, in the reign of his father Constantine the Great. This tends to prove that at least some part of the fifth legion was stationed at Camboritum at that period. No. 2 is imperfect owing to the upper part of the stone being lost.

The following are accurate copies of the Inscriptions:

No. 1.	No. 2.
IMPCAES	LISSI
FLAVI	MVS
C..S.ANTINO	CAESAR
VLEG	
CONST	
ANTI	
NOPIO	
NOBCA	
S	

It is highly desirable that these interesting Inscriptions should be placed in a safer position than that which they now occupy.

2. OLD BRIDGE AT CAMBRIDGE.—Mr Benjamin Bevan, son of the engineer who superintended the erection of the present Great Bridge, has kindly placed in my hands some of his father's papers relative to its erection, which took place in the year 1823. This bridge was preceded by one of stone erected in 1754, and which was itself the successor of a series of wooden bridges replacing each other from a period closely succeeding if not preceding the Norman conquest. It is stated already (p. 5) that in 1754 Mr Essex saw the foundations of an ancient round-arched stone bridge when excavating for the bridge of stone erected by him. Mr Essex's bridge was removed in 1823 to make way for the present iron bridge. In digging down to the foundation of the south abutment on Sept. 26, 1823, Mr A. Browne, the contractor, found it to be "very different from that on the north side; it is one course of stone deeper than that, and the stone and masonry is laid on two courses of bond timber (laid across each other), each about 6½ or 7 inches thick by 13 or 14 inches wide. The timbers in each course are laid close to each other, and form an uniform mass of timber about 13 inches thick under the whole abutment.....I think there are no piles under

it. It is 9 feet 11 inches from the high water-mark to the bottom
of the stone-work, and about 11 feet to the bottom of the lowest
course of timber. The soil under the old abutment, and where we
are excavating for the new part [the new bridge is wider than the
old one], is as strong and firm a gault as I have ever seen, without
any springs of water in it, as on the other side" (*Letter from Mr A.
Browne to B. Bevan, Esq.*, dated 26 Sept. 1823). On the 29th
and 30th of September Mr Bevan was at Cambridge, and a minute
of his instructions shows that he left the old bed of timber undisturbed, merely extending it so as to form a foundation large enough
for the new bridge. He states that he "found the planks spiked
down very firm," and "the lower course of hewn Totternhoe stone
set on a thin course of about 3 inches of clay."

It is not clear to what date this timber foundation ought to
be referred, but it has appeared desirable to record its existence.
Totternhoe is in Bedforshire, and not far from the *Icknield Way*,
and therefore possessing an easy means of communication with
Cambridge from a very early period.

3. KING'S HEDGES.—A re-examination of the camp by the side
of the *Akeman Street* at the place called King's Hedges has caused
me to have still more doubt concerning its Roman origin than was
the case when the remark given in the body of this treatise (p. 10)
was written. On the side bounded by the Roman Road a large
ditch was perhaps not to be expected, but upon the other sides there
must undoubtedly have been one if it was of Roman origin. Scarcely
any traces of large external ditches are now to be seen; such may,
nevertheless, have been there; for the embankment, which has been of
enormous width, is now so much lowered by the removal of the soil
as to be throughout the greater part of its extent only faintly traceable. The camp is situated in a quite level country, and is large
enough to have been the site of a Roman station; whereas if belonging to that people it can hardly have been more than a *castrum
æstivum*. If a Norman work its size is not an objection, for the
armies of that period, consisting chiefly of cavalry, required a very
large space relatively to their number. Careful measurements give
the following dimensions for this encampment:

Length parallel to the Akeman Street   .   .   .   738 yds.
Width   295
Thickness of the embankment in the best preserved parts 13

The corners are rectangular.

4. ARBURY.—This camp is nearly of the shape of a flat, four-centred arch, and is almost destroyed by the plough. The chord of the arc is quite obliterated. As far as can now be determined, it was probably about 286 yards in length. It is impossible to determine the width, from the bank having been quite removed in its middle part. The ditch has entirely disappeared.

INDEX.

76

Erming Street, 31
Exning, 39, 40
Fen Road, 41
Fleam Dyke, 60
Fleet, 45
Foxton, 38
Fulbourn, 21
Galley Hill, 55
Gedney Hill, 45
Giant's Hill, 50
Glassmore, 43
Godmanchester, 31
Granta, 7
Grantabrigge, 7
Grantchester, 25
Grunty Fen, 11
Haddenham, 46
Haregate, 53
Haydon, 64
Haydon Ditch, 63
Henxwell, 36
Hergate, 53
Hey Hill, 13
High Doles, 45
Holywell, 47
Horsey Bridge, 67
Horsheath, 23
How's House, 23
Iceanum, 39
Iciani, 9
Icknield Way, 33, 35
Itineraries of Antoninus, 8
King's Delph, 68
King's Hedges, 10, 73
Lidgate, 46
Limbury Hill, 37
Limlow Hill, 37
Linton, 23
Litlington, 36
Maney, 43
March, 41, 52
Mareway, 13, 39
Mildenhall, 39
Moat's Way, 48
Mutlow Hill, 40

Newmarket Heath, 40
Newton, 52
Old Causeway Dyke, 44
Old course of rivers, 68
Ousden, 46
Pampisford Ditch, 62
Peddar Way, 38, 39
Port Way, 14, 39
Rampton, 53
Reche, 60
Ring Hill, 39
Rivers, old course of, 68
Roads : Akeman Street, 10
—   — Street, near Tring, 17
—   Aldreth Causeway, 48
—   Ashwell Street, 35
—   Bishops Stortford to
        Braughing, 41
—   Bullock Road, 54
—   Bury to Spalding, 51
—   Cambridge to Braughing, 30
—   Cambridge to Chesterford,
        30
—   Cnut's Dyke, 58
—   Ely to Spalding, 44
—   Erming Street, 31
—   Fen Road, 41
—   Mr Woodward's
        opinion concerning, 43
—   Grantchester and Barton,
        24
—   Icknield ·Way, 33
—   Mr Woodward's
        opinion concerning, 35
—   Mare Way, 13, 39
—   Moat's Way, 48
—   Peddar Way, 38
—   Mr Woodward's
        opinion concerning, 39
—   Port Way, 14, 39
—   Sand Way, 50
—   Sawtry Way, 45
—   Stangate, 31
—   Street Way, 38
—   Suffolk Way, 45

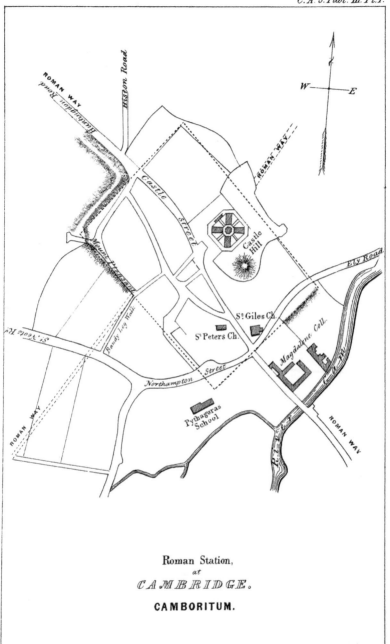

Roman Station,
at
CAMBRIDGE.

CAMBORITUM.

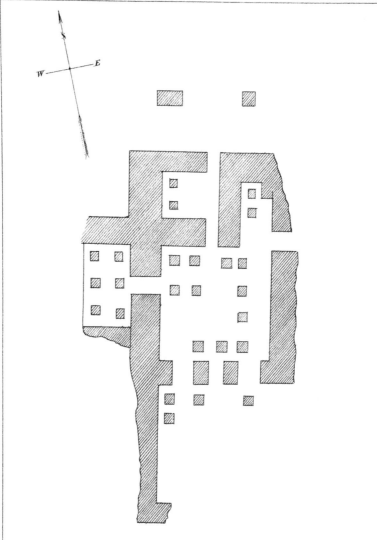

Roman Villa,
below
COMBERTON CHURCH,
from a Drawing by the Rev. J. J. Smith, M.A.
Scale ⅙ in. to a foot.

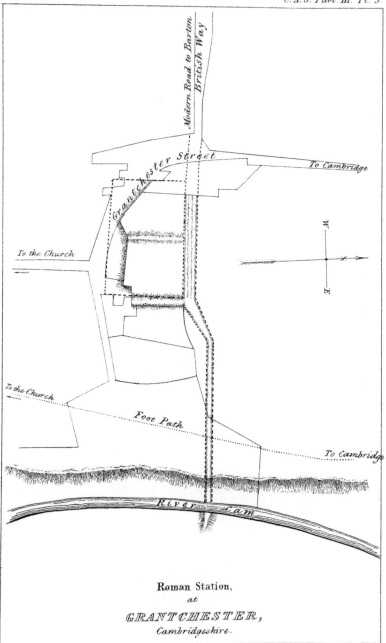

Roman Station,

at

GRANTCHESTER,

Cambridgeshire.

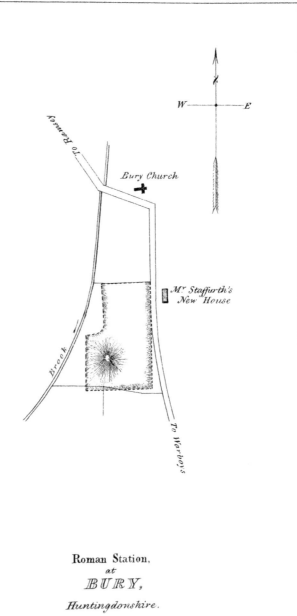

W——E

To Ramsey

Bury Church

Mr Staffurth's
New House

Brook

To Warboys

Roman Station,
at
BURY,
Huntingdonshire.

Metcalfe & Palmer, Lithog.rs

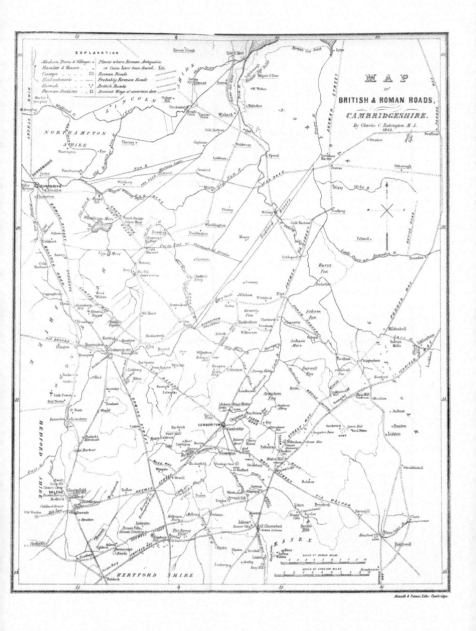

For EU product safety concerns, contact us at Calle de José Abascal, 56–1°, 28003 Madrid, Spain or eugpsr@cambridge.org.

www.ingramcontent.com/pod-product-compliance
Ingram Content Group UK Ltd.
Pitfield, Milton Keynes, MK11 3LW, UK
UKHW012336130625
459647UK00009B/328